QUILTS OF ILLUSION

FRONTISPIECE: Tumbling Blocks (Cross variation) pattern pieced quilt, c. 1850, Warren County, Kentucky. Made by Margaret Calvert. 77″ x 72″. Silk, cotton, wool, and mohair. (*Collection The Kentucky Museum, Western Kentucky University; photo courtesy The Kentucky Quilt Project.*)

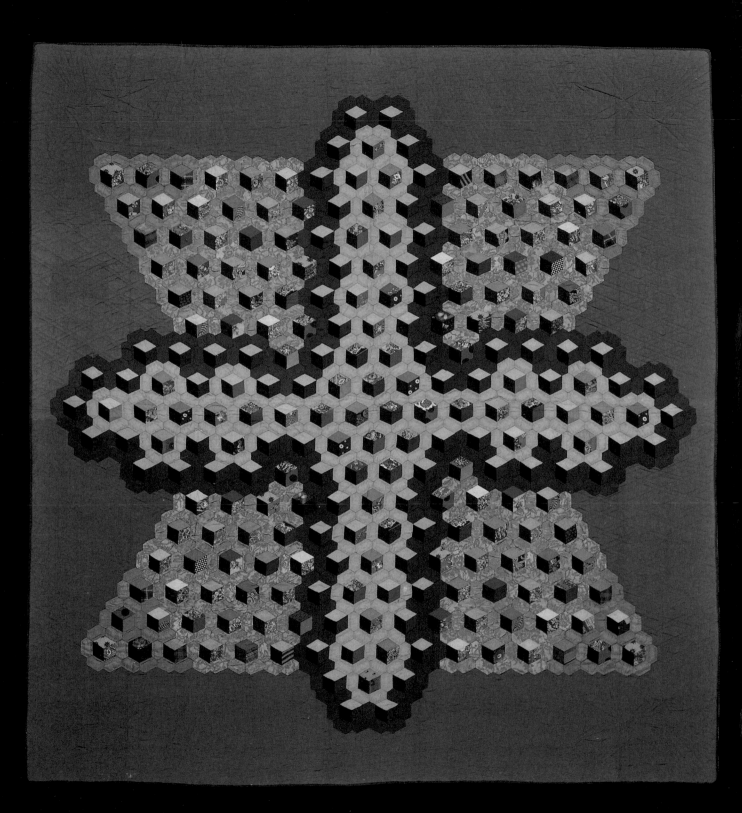

QUILTS OF ILLUSION

Tumbling Blocks, Delectable Mountains,

Stairway to Heaven, Log Cabin,

Windmill Blades, and

Other Optical

Designs

LAURA FISHER

A Sterling/Main Street Book
Sterling Publishing Co., Inc.   New York

Dedicated to Gary with thanks for his constancy and positive thinking, to Frances and Herman Fisher for their hope and support, and to the road not taken.

Library of Congress Cataloging-in-Publication Data

Fisher, Laura, [date]
  Quilts of Illusion.
  Bibliography: p.
  Includes index.
  1. Quilts, American. 2. Quilts—United States—
History—19th century. 3. Quilts—United States—History
—20th century. 4. Optical illusion in art. I. Title.
NK9112.F57   1987   746.9′7′0973   87-5653

Cover and text design by Frank Mahood

10 9 8 7 6 5 4 3 2 1

A Sterling / Main Street Book

Published 1990 by Sterling Publishing Company, Inc.
387 Park Avenue South, New York, N.Y. 10016
© 1988 by Laura Fisher
Distributed in Canada by Sterling Publishing
% Canadian Manda Group, P.O. Box 920, Station U
Toronto, Ontario, Canada M8Z 5P9
Distributed in Australia by Capricorn Ltd.
P.O. Box 665, Lane Cove, NSW 2066

Printed in Hong Kong
All rights reserved

Sterling   ISBN 0-55562-009-4

CONTENTS

PREFACE

OUR EYES LOOK, but our minds see. . . .

An optical illusion fools the eye. Scientifically, it is a visual experience in which a discrepancy exists between what we perceive and the real physical characteristics before us. Quilts, forms that are essentially planar, or two-dimensional, become illusionary when their design appears three-dimensional. Through touch, we acknowledge the quilt's flat surface, but in our mind's eye, we sense differing psychic effects—a kinetic pattern, multiple layers, or several designs seeming to occupy the same space simultaneously. Here is more than initially meets the eye.

The literature of quilting has taught us to appreciate antique American quilts first as historical and social artifacts, and more recently as fine art, remarkable and pleasing for their graphic images, the relationship between and manipulation of form, color, and line, and the presentation of repeated or sequential images. Antique illusionary quilts invite a fresh analysis, for they present what is by now familiar in unfamiliar, often enigmatic, ways. They challenge us to try to interpret ambiguity: are the patterns reaching out toward us or away from us? Are the lines straight or curved, connected or separate? Are we looking at designs from above or below? Are we seeing openwork layers? Is the surface raised or depressed? Such bedcovers affect our perception by dispelling familiar notions of such fundamental concepts as near and far, right and left, above and below. In many examples included in this book, these concepts are inter-changeable, presenting an altered vision that can be read in more than one way. For example, familiar series of squares, triangles, or rectangles often exhibit a shift in direction, a suggestion of volume or space, or the illusion that several designs are at play simultaneously—all through the manipulation of shape and color.

Many types of illusions exist, generated mostly through the use of angular shapes and strong tonal contrasts. In some illusionary quilts, a sense of space is conveyed by varying the size, color, and shape of some pieces; by interrupting a logical or expected pattern of alignment; or by placing shapes in unexpected and unconventional relationships. Other quilts include sections (called pattern blocks) which read individually as flat planes, but, when combined and multiplied, generate design elements that seem to exist on several levels. In still others, forms that can stand alone as distinct images—a star, a tree, a flower—produce kinetic, complex optical designs when combined. Often, the juxtaposition of light and dark alone conveys a sense of movement as lines appear to waver and elements seem to advance or recede. Different areas demand recognition all at the same time. Layers build, lines shift, forms pop out and disappear.

Optical illusion quilts are compelling because they vary from the norm and they vary within themselves. Their designs involve the viewer intellectually, not just aesthetically, by disturbing the accustomed confined space of a simple bed-cover, making it active, mysterious, and unpredictable. In many cases, the viewer cannot control what he or she is seeing. Many of these quilts gain optical impact from their negative, as well as their positive, spaces. The negative is the field between the pieced (the positive or designed) segments, typically of solid color or configuration. Although quiltmakers probably treated this aspect as a suitable background for the piecework, from the viewer's perspective it gains dominance, disturbing our understanding of the quilt, but in a stimulating, intriguing way.

For the needleworker of old, quiltmaking was all about *imagination*. The challenge was always to organize a group of scraps or small pieces into a whole cloth of pleasing appearance as well as utility. To me, antique illusionary quilts represent perhaps the most captivating exercise of the quiltmaker's need for self expression. Undoubtedly, many were constructed without a knowledge of perspective, of mechanical drawing, or the use of specialized tools to facilitate the task of design. In them is expressed a freedom of spirit and lack of restraint. Yet at the same time they required considerable thought, precise handling, and enviable concentration. Such quilts could not have been made in a hurry. Highly personal and individualized, even in the simplest patterns, their execution offered quiltmakers the opportunity to explore ideas and test designs. What commitment, perhaps even obsession, enabled quilters to plan, count, coordinate materials, then cut, count, and stitch to ensure that the whole would come out right? The attention to detail in these examples must have been intensely different from that of quilts made of just enough pretty blocks to yield a beautiful bedcovering. Many optical illusion quilts cannot be called beautiful in the conventional sense. To quilt lovers accustomed to visual presentations of tiny stitches and serene images, these quilts may appear chaotic or confused. Such confusion exists only in the viewer's perception, not in the construction of the design.

When I solicited collectors, dealers, and curators for quilts to include here, they first located examples of illusions among the classic Tumbling Blocks and Log Cabin variations. Often, bold graphics alone were considered to be optical illusions. Asked how quiltmakers managed to create such complex designs in a time of limited technical knowledge and design training, these experts replied, "serendipity," "luck," "chance," or "accident," coupled, of course, with innate artistic skill. Some felt that the existence of such designs must reflect a mathematical or geometrical education or inclination, while others insisted that most designs were simply the result of tinkering with small pieces of cloth with no awareness that a masterpiece would emerge. Happily for us, those artists had imagination, which allowed them to explore in fabric what today a painter or sculptor might create. And they had courage, which allowed them to defy conventional standards of taste and beauty to pursue the abstract fantasies of their mind's eyes.

As in other visual arts, the creator had to confront the issue of organization, or how to make sense of the patches. Some quilts illustrated here include thousands of pieces so intensely composed that viewers may be unable to decipher what they are seeing. The density of piecing greatly affects our ultimate perception, as do the relationships among colors employed. But even in simple two-color compositions that repeat a single form, provocative illusionary results are possible.

All of these examples have an order, but it may not be apparent at first glance. After the initial stunning impact, the elements can be dissected and the composition analyzed and understood. In none of the chosen quilts is there a pattern element that is unique to illusionary quilts. Their familiar forms—a square, a hexagon, a strip—appear countless times in everyday quilts. Their distinction as intriguing designs stems from the creative interaction of form, color, and pattern, and their consequent transformation into large, abstract surfaces.

This exploration of quilts of illusion encompasses several chapters. First is an explanation of the dynamics of these quilts: the quiltmaking traditions; principles of design and composition in art and needlework; perceptions and perspectives that color our appreciation of the designs; the types of visual illusions, and the forms with which they have been created. The second chapter reviews historical inspirations that might have influenced the appearance of optical illusions in American quilts, such as motifs in ancient textiles, woodwork, tile work, and architectural ornamentation. The third chapter is a portfolio of optical illusion quilts, organized by the basic geometric shape used to construct the design. A final chapter presents four examples of optical illusion quilts—a Tree of Life, a Tumbling Blocks, Three-Dimensional Fans, and an Eccentric Star—for readers to reproduce or modify to create their own illusions.

Each viewer has options for examining the quilts illustrated in this book, for everyone brings along a host of past experiences—an ability to judge size and distance; habits of seeing; knowledge of art and design; processes of perception; and even the unique physical properties of your own eyes. The illusions presented here may be more apparent, therefore, to some people than to others.

Take your time examining the quilts, at least enough for the natural process of vision fatigue to cause a shift in image. Most examples increase in complexity and kinetic illusion with concentrated attention. Turn the book sideways and up-side down. Explore the effects of a difference in perspective or light source upon the patterns. Look first at the dominant form or forms from which each design is constructed, using them as a visual point of reference as the motifs begin to shift and as elements emerge and recede. Then concentrate on a different aspect—for example, the light or dark field, the center block, or the ellipse—and let yourself be mystified, and I hope delighted, by all you see. Look for repeating elements, or the common denominator, such as the star, the triangle, or a strip of a certain color or tone. When you mentally dissect the quilt surfaces, greater appreciation for their remarkable qualities will follow.

I consider this study a beginning, for it is only recently that quilts have been acknowledged as the visual precursors of many of the design "innovations" and color systems that were later employed by practitioners of Op Art and other con-temporary painting. Although many of our examples are of the nineteenth cen-tury in materials, patterning, construction, and cultural sensibility, their designs are compatible with the most contemporary home or corporate environment. As collectors hang their antique patchwork "Eschers" and "Vasarelys" alongside modern paintings, the optical illusion quilt is bound to achieve its rightful place in art history.

As sensory beings, we delight in visual trickery, often seeking optical stimula-tion from such relatively modern innovations as 3-D movies, strobe lights, and holograms. These illusionary quilts, far older, are as remarkable and enticing a visual experience.

1.

THE DYNAMICS OF ILLUSION

Antique American quilts, long revered as our most colorful naïve folk art, have a familiar form and construction. Quilts of illusion employ that form, but present it with an unfamiliar face. They are mysterious and intriguing, offering multiple images, a rich unity of opposites, visually dynamic spatial forces, a sense of movement, and constant visual stimulation—all within the familiar confines of a bed-sized expanse of fabric. The three-dimensional visual appearance of these flat, two-dimensional forms led to the development of *Quilts of Illusion*.

In its early years, quiltmaking was considered a craft. Young ladies and even young men were taught basic sewing skills in order to make bedcovers for colonial families. Over the years, the artistic possibilities of the craft became increasingly refined and a native folk art was developed as quilters invented more and more patterns to utilize their precious scraps of fabric. In so doing, needleworkers tested combinations of color, shape, and design, spurred by an innate sense of creativity.

The fascinating, inherently graphic content of antique quilts was brought to the attention of a wide contemporary audience at a landmark 1971 exhibition at New York's Whitney Museum, "Abstract Design in American Quilts." The exhibition's organizers, Jonathan Holstein and Gail van der Hoof, helped to alter our perspective on these textile treasures by presenting them as significant works of art.

Quilts of illusion have more in common with the art of the twentieth century than they do with other historic American textiles. Few of the quilts illustrated in this book have the charm or quaint sentimentality of friendship or album quilts, the historic content of presentation or commemorative quilts, or the beautiful needlework of appliqué quilts, acknowledged quilt heirlooms that have been cherished from one generation to the next and often exhibited in prestigious museums.

Illusion quilts are generally patchwork mosaics, incorporating many pieces organized by shape and color into a harmonious whole. That so many have survived to this day is remarkable when one considers that the humble patchwork quilt (in contrast to the special occasion appliqué) was created for everyday household use, and rarely intended to be treasured for posterity. The intricacy with which many were composed suggests, however, that their makers took special pride in the skillful execution of the fabric bits and never actually used the finished quilts.

While many of these bedcovers have the appearance and construction of utilitarian quilts, their designs are anything but ordinary. In many examples, little stars "pop", octagons "float", lines zigzag, blocks tumble and twist, and designs seem to move in and out of the quilts' flat surfaces. As early Kentucky quiltmaker Aunt Jane best expressed it: "How much piecin' a quilt is like livin' a life. You can give the same kind o' pieces to two persons, and one will make a Nine Patch and one will make a Wild Goose Chase, and they will be two quilts made out of the same kind of pieces and jes' as different as they can be. And that is jes' the way with livin'. The Lord sends us the pieces, and we can cut them out and put them together pretty much to suit ourselves, and there is a

FIG. 1.1. Right Angles Patchwork pattern pieced quilt top detail, c. 1875, Midwest. Maker unknown. 90″ x 72″. Cotton. An extraordinary sense of solidity, volume, and depth is conveyed in this rarely seen pattern. The "Y" shape seen so clearly in this detail is repeated hundreds of times across the quilt surface. It has been created by joining three identical L-shaped or chevron pieces. To understand the construction of this design, think of cubes whose diamond-shaped sides have been clipped at the centers to allow the insertion of a neighboring element, making a composition that is perhaps more akin to Tumbling Blocks than quilt patterns which bear that title. The optical effect is like an aerial view, looking down into the space of a densely packed cityscape of calico high-rises. (*Author's collection.*)

11

heap more in the cuttin' out and the sewin' than there is in the caliker" (Hall and Kretsinger, *The Romance of the Patchwork Quilt in America*, 83).

Pieced quilts were always planned to some extent, as the seamstress determined what shape the elements would take and how many were needed to complete the bedcover. Occasionally, designs were sketched in advance and the fabric pieces laid out according to a plan. But other designs may have resulted as the quiltmaker played with colors, shapes, and patterns until a pleasing solution emerged. Organizing the pieces and blocks by color and line was one of the few creative outlets available to women in the heyday of quiltmaking, yet there is a consensus among quilt experts that any design planning was limited to the preparation of the individual pattern blocks and that no quiltmaker could have planned the extraordinary optical illusions which enliven the surfaces of the most kinetic examples.

Many quilters worked from patterns, either directly copying design and color, or applying a personal creative touch to prepare an unusual example. Quilt patterns, both classic and novelty designs, were available commercially and could be swapped with neighbors, copied, or purchased directly from newspapers, periodicals, batting manufacturers, and even professional quilt designers. The quest for new designs was an integral part of the pleasure of quiltmaking and frequently led to the creation of beautiful quilts. It is unlikely, however, that instructions on how to compose some of the masterful illusions illustrated in this book were ever communicated through a pattern book or commercial source. In the earliest published books that discuss quilt patterns, there is little mention of the eye-dazzling potential of the designs, even for those patterns called "puzzle", the likeliest to generate "trick" results. Ruth Finley addresses the visual qualities of only a few of the hundreds of patterns described in *Old Patchwork Quilts and the Women Who Made Them*.

Until Jonathan Holstein's book, *The Pieced Quilt: An American Design Tradition*, very little had been written about the optical impact of quilts. But much had been reported about women's joy and excitement in exploring the art of patchwork. As Alice Morse Earle wrote in 1898, "Women revelled in intricate and difficult patchwork; they eagerly exchanged patterns with one another; they talked over the designs, and admired pretty bits of calico, and pondered what combinations to make, with far more zest than women ever discuss art or examine high art specimens today" (*Home Life in Colonial Days*, 271). She noted that, through quilting, "women were able to express their longing for decoration, their pride in needlework, and their love for color" (ibid., 26). Through social interchange, women learned how to improve their compositions' interest and appeal and were challenged to try out new patterns, all within the proper framework of making a useful household article.

Among the tens of thousands of quilts that have been stitched in America in the last two centuries, why do some display designs of illusion while others, using similar patterns and pieces, do not? For the illusionary quilts pictured here, their makers must have derived an intellectual and artistic pleasure in creating designs that exceeded the traditional goal of making a functional, attractive object.

As with other art forms like painting and sculpture, the quilt artist must have relied on standard principles of design composition, such as:

establishing a point of emphasis (figs. 1.12, 3.9 and 3.66);

creating an appearance of either perfect or imperfect balance; that is, countering a small area of full intensity with a large area of half intensity, or little with big, or solid with void (fig. 3.18);

establishing unity through a repetition of different elements (figs. 1.24, 1.25);

creating a rhythm that may be curvilinear, echoing, or repetitive (figs. 1.4, 1.6, 1.21);

establishing proportions of the parts to the whole by pre-determining the size and relative scale of the pattern elements (figs. 3.1, 3.10, and 3.24).

The quilter had to have been intuitively aware of those elements of organization which any artist employs to create a composition, including:

Line, the basic device to create form or define pattern. Even without including actual physical lines to indicate design, a quiltmaker can suggest lines through the edges of the pattern pieces, as in figures 1.12 and 4.1. Diagonal lines imply activity, movement, and direction, while verticals and horizontals generally are inactive. Countless examples here convey agitated linear effects because they include, or imply, diagonal lines.

Plane, or the location in visual space of any aspect of the design. The quilt artists inventing illusions have manipulated planes by including elements that appear parallel to the quilt surface, along with others that suggest depth or a third dimension because they are diagonal or curved, as in figures 1.11, 3.63, and 3.81.

Solids and voids, or masses and space, which suggest visual variety because they play something against nothing. Optical illusion quilts often suggest solids floating above a flat surface, convey a sense of occupied emptiness, or transform the ground into an imaginary occupied space, as in figures 3.15, 3.27, and 3.40.

Perspective, in which the relative size of the elements of the design seems increased or decreased. This can be either one-point, or linear, which gives the impression that all lines in a composition are parallel, receding, or will meet at a vanishing point (fig. 3.4); two-point, where the lines need not be parallel to the surface, but the foreground appears foreshortened to convey an illusion of depth (fig. 3.46); or aerial, in which imaginary lines in the distance are made smaller or lighter to sharpen the foreground (fig. 3.2).

Color, which has hue (the wavelength of reflected light); value (the amount of white or black present in or modifying the hue); and intensity (the saturation or transparency, depth, or lightness of the hue). The attributes or sensations of color are threefold: hue (color or shade); brightness (lightness or darkness, luminescence); and saturation (extent to which the color departs from a neutral gray).

To create an illusion, the quiltmaker would manipulate all those elements and create a somewhat formal composition which had a symmetrical, almost mathematical, structure that organized the size, position, and direction of the pattern elements. Because they were not structured, informal compositions like crazy quilts generally could not produce an illusion. When joining the patchwork pieces according to a pre-planned scheme, one quiltmaker might repeat the same block over and over to build a quilt surface (fig. 3.1), while another might vary the blocks, achieving an overall pattern from the interaction of various aspects of the blocks when they merge (fig. 1.6).

The quiltmaker had several choices when planning her composition: she might build up a repeat design in the "English" patchwork or "allover" method, joining identical geometric shapes continuously without first grouping them (fig. 3.93). Or, she could build a pattern in blocks or in strips, first combining a number of patches in a design and then joining these to create a larger surface (fig. 3.95).

The most extraordinary examples of optical illusion quilts began to develop from the mid-nineteenth century onward, as block-work quilts became the preferred American system for construction, supplanting the

FIG. 1.2. Album Patch pattern pieced quilt, Amish, c. 1930, Mifflin County (Nebraskan Community), Pennsylvania. Maker unknown. 92″ x 84″. Cotton. The eye gets no rest in studying this illuminated composition of four-patch corner blocks, nine-patch center blocks, and fence-rail framework. A coral cotton grid seems to cross tessellated squares which read as octagonal green forms. Verticals and horizontals direct the eye to coral X's, which compete for attention with the nervous dark green outlines beneath (or are they above?) the delicate crisscross grid that links together all this energy. Where should one look first? (*Author's collection.*)

1.2

FIG. 1.3. Roman Stripe pattern pieced quilt, Amish, c. 1930, Holmes County, Ohio. Maker unknown. 80″ x 63½″. Cotton. In its vertical position, as shown, this vibrant quilt appears to contain black triangular tabs emerging from its surface, ready to be pulled to reveal an imaginary surprise. When viewed horizontally, black mountain peaks seem to progress up into a distant landscape amid a field of strips in desert sunset colors. The blacks vie for dominance with identically sized triangles pieced of narrow strips of pastels; together, these triangles read as shadowy diamonds that weave a mysterious diagonal pattern across the quilt surface. (*Photo courtesy Esprit Quilt Collection.*)

FIG. 1.4. Indiana Puzzle pattern pieced quilt, Amish, c. 1920, Indiana. Maker unknown. 82" x 70". Cotton. Here is the most direct form of illusion: a figure/ground, or positive/negative counterpoint in which the eye cannot decide if the light or dark forms are dominant. Although the pattern appears to be composed of gracefully interlocking curvilinear forms, in fact it is created with large center squares from which four triangles extend. The tiny four patches at the intersections read as sinuous extensions of the form because of the careful tonal coordination. (*Photo courtesy Esprit Quilt Collection.*)

FIG. 1.5. One Thousand Pyramids pattern pieced quilt, c. 1890, Pennsylvania. Maker unknown. 75" x 72". Cotton. An unseen force at the pinwheel center seems to be sucking the quilt surface into a vortex. Although triangles are typically straight sided, these give the illusion of having curvilinear sides receding inward. This effect is called a logarithmic spiral, wherein the distance between circles appears smaller toward the center. Conceivably, the quiltmaker could have prepared the design by drawing overlapping circles, adding lines to divide them, and creating patchwork pieces from the resulting diagram this way. Or the optical effect could have been the result of imprecisely cut pieces, which in most cases would distort the finished quilt, but in this case would only accentuate the optical illusion. This striking quilt is a later innovation of the colonial tradition which dictated that a young girl collect a thousand triangles of calico, after which she would meet the man who would become her husband. Here, the maker probably combined her patches first into eight larger triangles which were then united with their points facing inward. (*Collection of George Kiberd; photo courtesy Sandra Mitchell.*)

whole cloth quilt, the framed center medallion, and other early quilt formats. Quiltmakers found that the repetition of one block, or the combination of two or more different pieced blocks, could produce wonderful and often dramatic designs. (The block is traditionally a 10″ to 14″ square incorporating small patches of fabric cut to predetermined shape and varied in color and/or size.)

Blocks could be composed either symmetrically, that is, of uniformly shaped and arranged pieces; asymmetrically, incorporating diverse pieces; or split, that is, comprised of two equal parts (usually triangles) where half is a solid piece, and the other half combines smaller geometric pieces. According to Jonathan Holstein, "in the case of either symmetrical or asymmetrical blocks, it is extremely difficult to envision what the overall results will be from the contemplation of a single block" (*The Pieced Quilt*, 53). The quilter would find that making square symmetrical blocks meant to be linked would "always form the same pattern no matter how she would turn the blocks," but asymmetrical or split blocks could be combined to produce many different graphic designs "by varying their orientation within the format" (ibid.). It is likely that very striking and unanticipated designs resulted from the latter process.

In quilts that are illusionary, blocks are frequently joined together without the physical or visual separation of a sashing strip or a solid intervening ground block. This allows internal elements within the patterned

FIG. 1.6. LeMoyne Star and Four Patch pattern pieced quilt, c. 1890, Shawnee, Oklahoma. Shoshone Indian maker. 81″ x 68″. Cotton. Serial ranks of three-dimensional pattern seem to step up, and back, and up again in a unique combination of classic geometric shapes. This four-color scheme of diamond and square shapes unites patterns of stars, cubes, and four patches. Could the maker have anticipated this dramatic, constantly shifting optical illusion? Different motifs vie for attention when the quilt is viewed horizontally or vertically. Stars incorporating two diamond arms of each of the four colors become more or less visible; plateaus appear; cubes advance or recede; and hexagonal forms emerge as the quilt is studied. (*Author's collection.*)

FIG. 1.7. Tumbling Blocks (Cross variation) pattern pieced quilt, c. 1850, Warren County, Kentucky. Made by Margaret Calvert. 77" x 72". Silk, cotton, wool, and mohair. Perhaps the most extraordinarily dimensional of all the Tumbling Blocks patterns ever executed, the Cross variation achieves a remarkable, almost surreal illusion of cubes floating free above a cross which itself appears superimposed above an hourglass figure. All of the forms appear to be suspended above a separate field. This startling abstract creation was a hundred years before its time in artistic freedom, eliciting great curiosity about the motivation and artistic background of its creator and the meaning of its imagery. The three-dimensional sense which all Tumbling Blocks patterns convey is heightened here by underlying images which differ from the cubes. (*Collection The Kentucky Museum, Western Kentucky University; photo courtesy The Kentucky Quilt Project.*)

FIG. 1.8. Delectable Mountains pattern pieced quilt, c. 1890, locale unknown. Maker unknown. 80" x 79". Cotton. Contrasting triangles are arranged in a composition that reverberates to the outer edges of the dramatic design. It appears as if six squares of decreasing size have been layered atop sawtooth grounds. In addition, a large crisscross form pulsates outward diagonally like an artist's rendition of radio waves. In reality, there are no layers. The quilt design has been organized by adding a sawtooth element to each row, implying a line that links the bases of those forms and tricks the viewer into thinking that separate planes of pattern exist. The design suggests activity radiating beyond the perimeter of the quilt. (*Photo courtesy Darwin D. Bearley.*)

Fig. 1.9. Touching Stars (String Star variation) pattern pieced quilt, c. 1900, Berks County, Pennsylvania. Maker unknown. 81″ square. Wool. Bold diamonds set in contrasting squares appear to be the predominant pattern around which this quilt was composed. Closer study reveals a busily pieced version of a figure/ground dichotomy in which the background vies for attention with the actual pattern of touching stars. These stars, pieced like a crazy quilt, are also called String Stars or Log Cabin Stars because they are made up of narrow, irregular segments of scrap fabric. Because the star points "touch," the solid areas of fabric which form the field come forward instead as a distinct geometric element. (*Collection of Kelter-Malce.*)

1.9

Fig. 1.10. Hummingbird Star pattern pieced quilt, c. 1900, locale unknown. Maker unknown. 79″ x 72″. Cotton. A variety of visually competitive forms energizes this graphic composition. The major element appears to be pale diamonds with dark centers, but it is a challenge to decide what design dominates: is it the concave white forms caught at their four corners with dots? Or four-armed stars of dark elongated diamonds centered with matching dots? Or the octagonal forms surrounding white concave diamonds? It is endlessly intriguing to see how combinations of unusually pieced blocks are capable of generating different visual illusions. (*Photo courtesy Darwin D. Bearley.*)

1.10

1.11

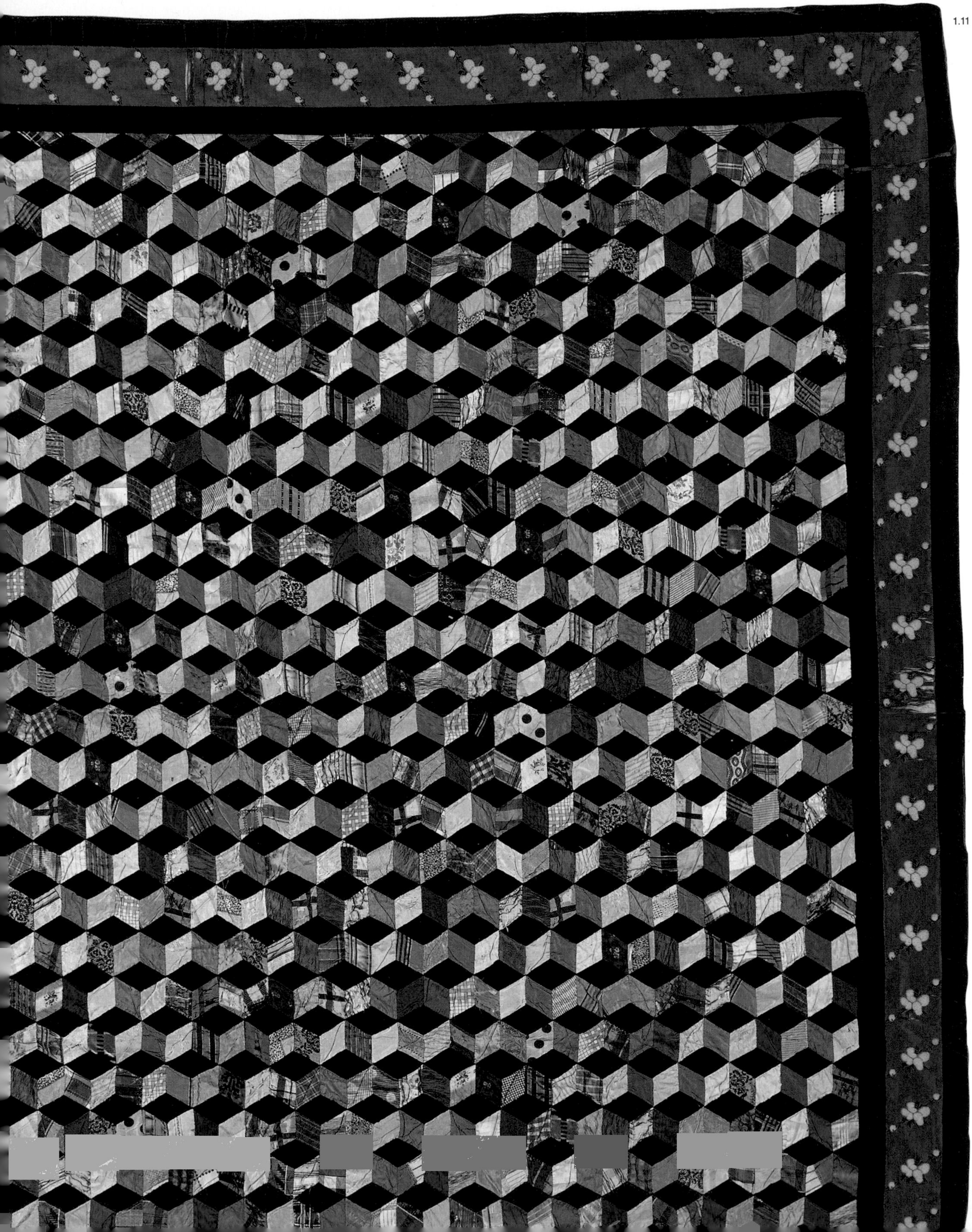

FIG. 1.11. Baby Blocks pattern pieced quilt, c. 1870, Queensboro, Kentucky. Made by Julia Wickliffe Beckham. 86" x 82". Silk and velvet. In this classically executed example of the Baby Blocks pattern, made by a woman who was the daughter, sister, and mother of governors of Kentucky and Louisiana, a solid velvet diamond shape constitutes what reads as both the top and bottom of cubes with patterned sides. Our perception shifts. We see cubes from above and below, as well as rows of patterned or solid fabric diamonds undulating like ribbons across the quilt surface. The placement of light, medium, and dark tones here has been carefully orchestrated to produce a flowing, elegant, three-dimensional surface design. (*Collection of the Owensboro, Kentucky Area Museum; photo courtesy The Kentucky Quilt Project.*)

FIG. 1.12 Thirty-nine Borders Enigma pattern pieced quilt, c. 1875, Pennsylvania. Maker unknown. 90" x 88". Cotton. Technically, this powerful graphic is a variation of the Single Log Cabin and "framed center" pattern formats. The main body of the quilt features concentric squares pieced of narrow strips which have been coordinated by color and print. The wider pieced borders were probably intended to hold the vibratory effect of the center in check, just as a Victorian frame would border a print. Instead, those borders emit their own dynamism because of their rich prints and contrasting lights and darks. The quilt's flat surface gives the illusion of receding inward toward a vanishing point, an illusion heightened by the imaginary line that appears at the mitered corners of the squares. The quilt's current owner, when asked her opinion of the maker's motivation, replied that "she probably felt trapped!" Viewers familiar with contemporary art may find the quilt startlingly like a Frank Stella painting. (*Collection of Susan Parrish.*)

blocks to "touch" or visually link and create additional lines of pattern across the quilt surface. In some examples, however, sashing adds visual strength to combined blocks, becoming a grid, at times dominant, at times subordinate, but always occupying a different visual plane than other aspects of the overall design. Some blocks can stand alone as images (fig. 3.55), but when combined may appear subordinate to new design elements (fig. 1.9). Other blocks form no clear design independently and must unite in order to create a geometric pattern (fig. 1.14).

Quiltmakers of old found they could create completely different surface designs using the same basic structure but shifting its position (fig. 3.6). While they may have been aware of the potential for creating the various patterns inherent in using asymmetrical blocks, most optical illusion designs were likely produced as happy accidents rather than as careful orchestrations. The interaction of color, contrast, and form might have been planned to some extent, but the kinetic impact of the final design was probably more fortuitous than anticipated.

1.12

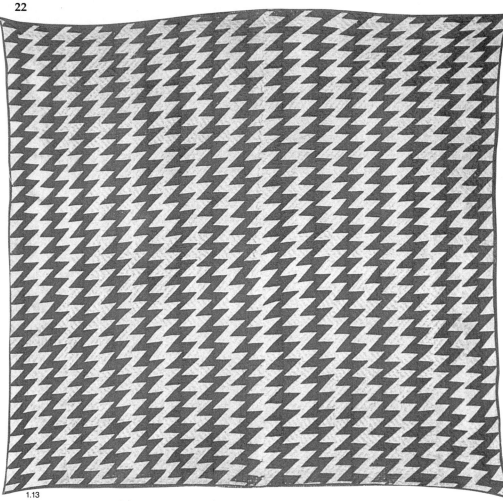

1.13

FIG. 1.13. Zigzag pattern pieced quilt, c. 1910, Pennsylvania. Maker unknown. Dimensions unavailable. Cotton. This classic figure/ground illusion in red and white is totally reversible. The viewer cannot decide if the dark or light (positive or negative) zigzag streak is dominant. A contemporary seamstress might think the quilt was composed of lengths of rickrack skillfully positioned to interlock. In reality, hundreds of identical rhomboids have been artfully combined to produce a crisp, dramatic abstraction whose stepped effect conveys a sense of motion and instability. (*Collection of Guernsey's.*)

FIG. 1.14. Log Cabin (Light and Dark variation) pattern pieced quilt detail, c. 1880, locale unknown. Maker unknown. Dimensions unavailable. Silk satin. This quilt detail illustrates how four small Log Cabin squares have been arranged so that the light triangular halves join at the intersection of four identical squares to create a larger diamond. Innumerable varieties of large-scale design are possible with the Log Cabin pattern, depending upon the juxtaposition or turning of the light and dark elements. (*Photo courtesy The Main Street Press.*)

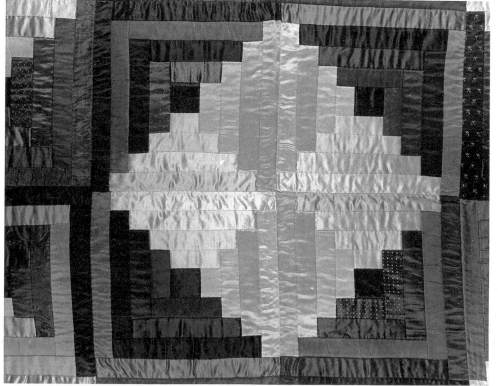

1.14

FIG. 1.15. Log Cabin (multiple variations) pattern pieced quilt detail, c. 1880, locale unknown. Maker unknown. Dimensions unavailable. Cotton. Three Log Cabin pattern variations—Barn Raising, Light and Dark, and Streak of Lightning—have been successfully combined on one surface using thousands of strips of fabric. Extraordinary attention to the organization of the light and dark pieces of the small Log Cabin blocks and to the rotation of those blocks resulted in a flawless geometric composition. (*Collection of Buckboard Antiques.*)

In many of these examples, the structural blocks disappear within the visual activity of the overall composition uniting them (fig. 3.71). In others, the block is readily identifiable but appears in the company of other complex design elements (fig. 1.2). A number of the illusions presented here are of form and shape, rather than color. In some, two pattern elements are perceived simultaneously (fig. 1.6) or merge into a new pattern (fig. 1.23). Some are spatial illusions, where one pattern is seen as existing above or below another (fig. 1.7).

Quilts of illusion appear vibrant, changeable, and intriguing because *the eye* may receive impressions, but *the mind* interprets them. Through various processes of perception, the viewer makes conclusions about the various optical clues of size, shape, position, direction, color, texture, and the forces transmitted by the patterns. Perception occurs, and differs, among people, always in the context of prior experiences, present circumstances, and visual abilities.

The Gestalt theory of psychology deals with the concept of perception and refers to the "whole," the "configuration," or the "form." It concludes that there are laws or principles of organization at work which show that how an object is perceived cannot be predicted just by adding up our knowledge of its parts, and that those parts may become unobservable when they are combined with other parts. This theory is the essence of illusionary quilts. Quilts of illusion are ambiguous: when the eye is stimulated by shape and line, more than one pattern can easily be seen. The different elements cannot be observed simultaneously; only one shape will predominate at any given moment, varying as our observation is prolonged. The immediately visible shape is called the figure; between it and the viewer is the ground, of indeterminate distance.

FIG. 1.16. Log Cabin (Light and Dark variation) pattern pieced quilt, c. 1880, locale unknown. Maker unknown. Dimensions unavailable. Wool. Through the consistent combination of the light and dark elements of the basic Log Cabin block, this classic pattern produces a totally reversible image—a positive/negative configuration—on the quilt surface. Four blocks are grouped with their dark triangular halves abutting so that the light halves also unite to form a similar large diamond element. Typically, the Log Cabin pattern allows the quilter to incorporate thousands of different scraps of fabric; the power of this simple graphic is accentuated by the limited selection of fabrics used to create the design. (*Collection of Avis, Flora, and Alex Skinner Medawar.*)

1.15

1.16

FIG. 1.17. Log Cabin (Barn Raising variation) pattern pieced quilt, c. 1860, locale unknown. Maker unknown. 68″ x 62″. Wool. The simple act of setting the Barn Raising configuration on an angle is in itself uncommon, but the more unusual achievements of this dazzling example lie in its illusions of visual texture, interwoven composition, and illuminated palette. Thousands of strips of gray, blue, and golden brown have been precisely coordinated to give the impression of bargello needlework, as if yarns had been sewn through a backing to build up the beveled-edge diamond lattice-work. Placing the lightest (gray) strips at the edges of the Log Cabin blocks has made these areas appear raised in contrast to the black diamonds at the center of each segment. The gray strips also link visually as a network of light thread claiming our attention at the same time as the golden concentric squares pulsate to the sawtooth borders of the quilt. (*Courtesy Dr. Robert Bishop; photo © Schecter Lee.*)

To enhance our enjoyment of illusionary quilts, it is helpful to know what factors might influence our perceptions of shape. As Julian Hochberg outlines them, the principal Gestalt laws are (1) "the smaller a closed region, the more it tends to be seen as figure;" (2) "objects that are close together tend to be grouped together;" (3) "areas with closed contours tend to be seen as figure more than do those with open contours;" (4) "the more symmetrical a closed region, the more it tends to be seen as figure;" and (5) the eye tends to see "that arrangement of figure and ground. . . which will make the fewest changes or interruptions in straight or smoothly curving lines or contours" (*Perception*, 87).

What does all this mean to the viewer of a quilt of illusion? As one tries to focus on a particular area to gain visual stability and to determine the pattern, the visual system will become fatigued, and there may seem to be: a sensation of shifting or overlapping images (fig. 1.21); a sensation of ambiguity in the figure/ground relationship (fig. 1.9); a visual tension which makes it hard to separate figure from ground (fig. 1.10); or a change in the orientation of the pattern which causes the viewer to read different spatial effects (figs. 3.46 and 3.85).

The delightful, often unanticipated, and almost unexplainable tricks of perception create several types of illusions:

Figure/ground illusions, where the mind cannot separate an object (figure) from its environment. The figure element has the principal shape and should exist visually some distance from the ground.

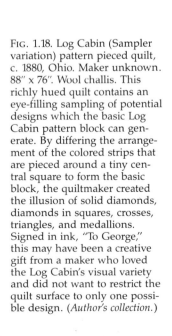

FIG. 1.18. Log Cabin (Sampler variation) pattern pieced quilt, c. 1880, Ohio. Maker unknown. 88″ x 76″. Wool challis. This richly hued quilt contains an eye-filling sampling of potential designs which the basic Log Cabin pattern block can generate. By differing the arrangement of the colored strips that are pieced around a tiny central square to form the basic block, the quiltmaker created the illusion of solid diamonds, diamonds in squares, crosses, triangles, and medallions. Signed in ink, "To George," this may have been a creative gift from a maker who loved the Log Cabin's visual variety and did not want to restrict the quilt surface to only one possible design. (*Author's collection.*)

1.18

FIG. 1.19. Double Wedding Ring pattern pieced quilt, c. 1935, Atlanta, Georgia. Maker unknown. 83½ x 71″. Cotton. This quilt's maker has produced a very different graphic from the classic Double Wedding Ring by using a bright (red) cotton fabric as the "ground" for her rings. As a result, the background looks as if it is the foreground, with its concave diamonds surmounting a field pieced of contrasting arched strips. The quilter fortified this visual trickery by placing a fabric of related, but not equal, tone within the elliptical areas between the ring curves. In traditional examples of this pattern, the ground and ellipses are usually white and thus typically read as subordinate to the pastel rings. (*Photo courtesy The Museum of American Folk Art; gift of Dr. Robert Bishop.*)

FIG. 1.20. Mosaic (Stars variation) pattern pieced quilt detail, c. 1860, Midwest. Maker unknown. 70″ square. Wool challis. Hexagonal "cells" or "rosettes" are linked like a honeycomb with hexagonally pieced triangular areas which together read as large-scale six-pointed stars. Using hexagons only, the quiltmaker manipulated two geometric forms to create a design of multiple images rather than of space or movement. The hexagon, although difficult to piece because some of its sides are cut on the bias, is nevertheless one of the most enduringly popular patches. (*Author's collection.*)

1.20

FIG. 1.21. Robbing Peter to Pay Paul pattern pieced quilt, Amish, c. 1904, probably Midwest. Maker unknown. 77″ x 65″. Cotton. An intense blue/green network of concave squares aligns diagonally across the quilt surface, while, simultaneously, glowing red circles form a similar network. Each set of forms competes for visual dominance in this figure/ground illusion. The pattern here is perceived as reversible; the eye focuses on neither element exclusively. To construct this complex pattern, the blocks are fashioned by carving off elliptical forms from each side and using those slivers as an element in the construction of the neighboring contrasting-colored block. This borrowing or sharing of design elements enhances the kinetic visual sensation of the design, as do the complementary colors used in this example. (*Photo courtesy Barbara S. Janos and Barbara Ross.*).

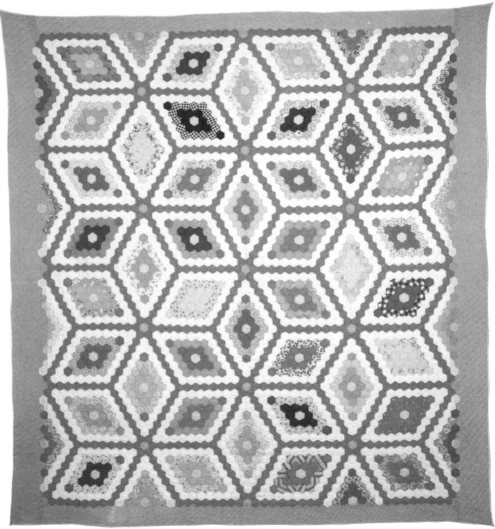

1.22

These illusions are perceived as reversible or equivocal relationships, in which the mind cannot choose between the positive or negative shapes and shifts attention repeatedly from one area to the other (figs. 1.3 and 1.21);

Closure illusions, where the viewer tends to perceive closed gaps or filled spaces where there are incomplete visual patterns (figs. 3.57 and 3.90);

Size and direction illusions, where there is a discrepancy between what we see and what is measurable fact. These can range from simple linear suggestions to complex superimposed images. Strong directional forces within a given pattern may alter our perception of the geometric shape at the core of that pattern (figs. 3.21 and 3.109);

Interrupted systems illusions, where space and depth are conveyed because the repeat or periodicity of certain pattern systems has been altered, or the logical flow has shifted in direction, thus introducing planes on a flat surface (figs. 3.24, 3.73, and 3.81);

FIG. 1.22. Rainbow Tile (Hexagons variation) pattern pieced quilt, c. 1920, probably Ohio. Maker unknown. 78″ x 74″. Cotton. Thousands of tiny hexagons have been grouped into diamond-shaped segments rather than the "Granny's Garden" rosette format with which quilt lovers are more familiar. These diamonds are then employed as in a Tumbling Blocks composition, creating large-scale cubes and stars that vie for visual dominance. This optical effect is called an illusion of pattern and periodic structure, in which geometric figures pop out or turn in with equal regularity as the quilt is observed. Lines of lavender hexagons direct the viewer's attention in all directions in this rollicking graphic illusion. (*Author's collection.*)

FIG. 1.23. Foundation Rose and Pine Tree pattern appliqué quilt, c. 1850, Carlisle, Pennsylvania. Maker unknown. 85″ square. Cotton. Mid-nineteenth-century floral appliqué quilts are rarely illusionary. They are prized instead for their needlework and representational qualities. Until the nation began to appreciate geometric design as "worthy" art (see chapter 2) this form of red and green appliqué was regarded traditionally as a "best" quilt. But in this dramatic creation, the floral imagery has become subordinate to the geometric illusions formed by the convergence of the appliqué blocks. Sharply pointed, propeller-like stars emerge from the luxurious appliqué work, as do four-pointed stars formed by the touching clusters of rounded shapes, while scalloped dots appear within octagonal forms. This multiplicity of design elements in visual competition, unusual in an appliqué quilt, rivals the best illusionary effect of geometric compositions. (*Photo courtesy Darwin D. Bearley.*)

FIG. 1.24. Flying Geese and Tudor Rose patterns pieced quilt, c. 1930, locale unknown. Maker unknown. Dimensions unavailable. Cotton. Two distinct pattern blocks have been alternated to produce a composition in which each pattern advances and recedes simultaneously. Using contrasting triangles, the quiltmaker arranged the Flying Geese elements to link across blocks set on point so that they read as a delicate horizontal and vertical grid above a patterned ground. Where triangles from the Geese blocks intersect matching corners of the Tudor Rose blocks, the viewer perceives a grid linking those blocks as well. (*Photo courtesy Frank Ames.*)

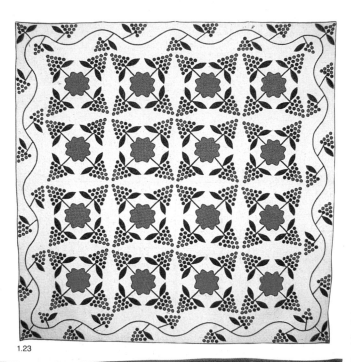

1.23

1.24

FIGS. 1.25, 1.26. Flo's Fan (New York Beauty variation) pattern pieced quilt details, c. 1925, Greene County, Tennessee. Made by Minnie Swatzel. 76½″ x 61½″. Cotton. This densely patterned quilt surface is a study in contrasts. Dramatic sawtooth circles appear to be whole, and also to rotate, as if anchored beneath a dark grid by a series of square bolts. The mechanical looking sawteeth seem to squeeze in toward the white squares, but the squares are strong enough visually to compete for the viewer's attention as they shift and pop up from their "curtained" frames. As the enlarged detail shows, the quilter's use of intricate patches—with pointed edges, curves, and diagonals, all expressing movement—gives the design great illusionary potential. (*Collection of Marjorie Armstrong; photos courtesy Quilts of Tennessee.*)

1.25

1.26

32

1.27

Pattern and periodic structure illusions, where a consistent geometric pattern may be small enough or viewed at such a distance as to be perceived as having a single color value, producing a variety of perceptual effects (figs. 3.20 and 3.26);

Distortion, where the viewer tries to focus to correct what is perceived as a visual aberration (figs. 3.5 and 3.42);

Brightness contrast illusions, where how light or dark a certain area seems depends upon comparison with surrounding areas of lighter or darker value (figs. 1.29 and 3.3);

Irradiation, where light and dark areas of equal size may be perceived as unequal because a white area is thought to produce a retinal image that affects the eye's receptors less selectively than a dark image (fig. 1.3).

In layman's terms, here is some of what you are likely to see as you study quilts of illusion. The quilt surfaces will appear activated; pattern elements will seem to shift or reverse themselves as you watch (fig. 3.115). Pattern blocks that were constructed of certain shapes will seem to

FIG. 1.28. Center Diamond pattern pieced quilt, Amish, c. 1910, Lancaster County, Pennsylvania. Maker unknown. 80" square. Wool. In this spectacularly colored diamond, the similarity in value and intensity between the two shades of pink wool blurs the distinction between the edge of the diamond and its surrounding field. The quilt surface appears to throb and radiate, the hallmark of the best Pennsylvania Amish quilts. This effect is intensified because the colors are complementary on the color wheel, a situation which can generate stunning optical tricks. (*Private collection, photo courtesy Barbara S. Janos and Barbara Ross.*)

FIG. 1.27. Double Four-Patch pattern pieced quilt, Amish, dated 1901, Holmes County, Ohio. Maker unknown. Dimensions unavailable. Cotton. The entire quilt surface seems to implode and explode simultaneously. The viewer's focus shifts from the suggestion of a deep, dark "background" to a lighter "foreground" grid conveyed by the linkage of the pieced double four-patch pattern blocks. A constant visual tension has been expressed through the decision to place the pattern blocks on point, creating a shadowy zigzag inner border that appears to throb at the edges of the body of the quilt, where the similarity in tone of some of the squares in the smaller four patches to the larger black squares has caused the red and camel elements to "float" above the darker ground. (*Collection of Barbara S. Janos and Barbara Ross.*)

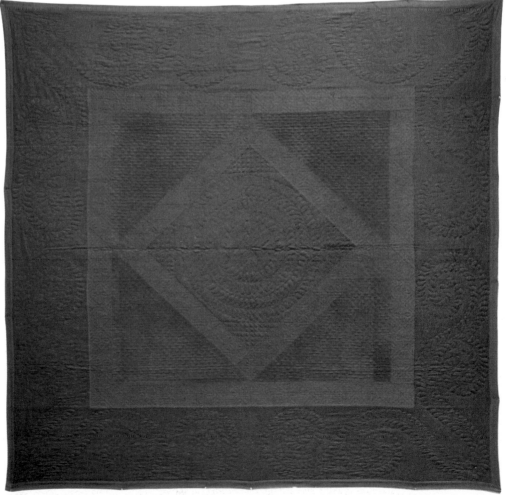

1.28

FIG. 1.29. Crown of Thorns pattern pieced quilt, Amish, c. 1915, Indiana. Maker unknown. 80″ x 76″. Cotton. The same pattern pieces of strips and triangles comprise each of the twenty blocks in this quilt, yet the blocks read as very different designs because of the juxtaposition of contrasting or complementary fabric pieces within each block. Some look like curved squares with pointed extensions; others, like crosses within diamonds, as "T" formations, or as combinations of these variations within each block. The changing images result from either the contrast between light and dark pieces or from the similarity in value of the pieces to their surrounding field or to contiguous patches. (*Photo courtesy Darwin D. Bearley.*)

disappear or to be transformed into other shapes (fig. 1.10). And, most remarkably, space will loom out at or back from the viewer, even though we all know we are looking at flat surfaces. Elements within the quilts will seem to advance or recede, to switch from left to right, or to be visible from above or below. That is what most illusion quilts portray; they express space on flat planes which do not overlap.

Only appliqué quilts have physically overlapping elements (layered flower petals, for example), yet very few of them exhibit surface designs which qualify as illusionary. The several examples in chapter 3 (figs. 3.88, 3.101, and 3.102) convey illusions through the manipulation of their negative spaces.

Quilts of illusion are not collages, nor are they three-dimensional in reality, yet they communicate a sense of volume or space through the skillful manipulation of color and shape. In some, a change in a logically anticipated sequence of pieces, such as a reversal or a tilt in angle, is enough to create a perception of imbalance or volume (fig. 3.62).

Diagonal lines, whether actual or implied, draw the eye along their length and imply depth or height. They are more difficult to handle in quiltmaking because they are usually cut on a bias to the grain of the fabric, giving them the potential to stretch out of shape and distort the alignment of the quilt surface. They convey depth by implying outward or inward motion or variation in plane. Planes may become apparent because some aspects of a sequential design merge in our perception as inclined lines (fig. 1.12).

Contrasting elements, whether of color or scale, may appear to float off the surface in an illusionary quilt (fig. 3.15). Lights and darks, whether black and white or contrasting colors, constitute positive and negative spaces which are primary generators of illusions. Many of these quilts depend on their inner spaces—the field or ground—to evoke the illusion. This use of reverse or contrasting value also conveys an illusion of movement or space (fig. 3.117). Even where the light and dark tonal contrasts may not be "pure," as in the case of patterns incorporating many different scraps of fabric in related tones, the eye manages to compensate for irregularities in sequence so that the optical effect is carried through.

Contrast also helps to create illusions where heavy grids appear to dominate patterns which are actually the pieced blocks constituting the primary design elements (fig. 3.3). Several examples here show a grid, either through the unification of sashing elements—the strips bordering the blocks (fig. 1.2)—or through our perception of a linkage of design elements within neighboring pieced blocks (fig. 3.8).

All grids appear to exist on different planes from the patterned quilt surfaces; some are dominant (fig. 3.111), while some are mysteriously subordinate (fig. 3.26). Designs based on grids actually emphasize the patterned motifs because of their clear geometrical structure.

Other quilt patterns gain a sense of illusion from repetition, either of forms scaled to fit within themselves (fig. 3.93), or of hundreds and even thousands of patches (figs. 3.34 and 3.39). Repetition creates a rhythmic patterning which exaggerates the geometric order and clarifies the visual field. The continuity of shape or color in rows causes the eye to follow a network of pattern (figs. 3.4, 3.39, and 3.41).

Finally, some of the most mysterious illusions are those in which the apparent visual pattern looks as if it is sharing pieces with the neighboring blocks. Yet in terms of the actual construction of the quilt, this could never occur (fig. 3.85). Certain elements, such as an elliptical leaf, a pine tree, or an elongated diamond, read as if they occupy two places at once. This results from the skillful piecing of blocks with many geometric shapes, and from the direct annexation of each block to its neighbor. As the size of such antique quilt surfaces increased, it is a wonder that their makers could actually have completed some of these extraordinarily eye-dazzling compositions.

2.

A HISTORY OF ILLUSION- ARY FORMS

FIG. 2.1. Star of the East pattern pieced quilt, Old Order Amish, c. 1930, Holmes County, Ohio. Maker unknown. 75" x 66". Cotton sateen. Using the sparest of forms and materials, the maker of this simple yet eloquent quilt has communicated a variety of optical illusions that suggest a lesson in plane geometry. Each of the star's six points appears as a solid three-dimensional form whose peaked edge advances towards the viewer. The effect is like looking down upon pyramidal volumes composed of light and electric blue tetrahedrons. The alternation of color in each point conveys the impression of a light source originating simultaneously from the upper right and lower left—each arm appears half in light and half in shadow. This strict alternation makes the star appear to rotate towards the light. Perhaps the drama of the finished quilt was anticipated; the quiltmaker could have experimented by folding a piece of paper, as in Japanese origami, and placing it on a dark ground. (*Collection of Morgan Anderson; photo courtesy Toli Pappas Photography.*)

THE OPTICAL ILLUSIONS present in these vibrant, extraordinary American quilts may have had as their inspiration styles that originated in other cultures and other eras. The growth of the United States in the eighteenth and nineteenth centuries brought immigrants who carried with them the crafts, concepts of design, and artistic traditions of their native lands to enliven and transform their new domestic environments.

The earliest American quilts reflected the fashions and tastes of Europe. Standards of beauty and design were narrowly proscribed. Two quilt formats prevailed: the center medallion, or framed center, which featured an appliqué motif often cut from naturalistic printed cottons and centered within multiple borders; and the simple block-work or one-patch variations incorporating squares of different fabrics. As the nineteenth century progressed, divisions and subdivisions of the pieced format ensued, leading to the extensive vocabulary of quilt patterns now regarded as an American design legacy. Few of these classic quilts are illusionary, however.

The distinctly American style of quiltmaking produced a broad range of recognizable, reproducible patterns that Sandi Fox considers "the common denominator of American culture in a constantly evolving environment." The representative quilt produced, she writes, was one "of challenge as well as circumstance, and it was stitched by rich and poor alike. The challenge was to take the lines of a pattern that had been worked by a thousand other hands and through dimension, color, and craftsmanship, make it uniquely one's own. It was a challenge well met, and in the doing, perhaps America's greatest glory" (*19th Century American Patchwork Quilt*, n.p.).

Quilt historians regard the explosion of patterns and styles in the nineteenth century as reflecting the genesis of an American identity from the multitude of ideas, cultures, and inventions brought by newcomers to our vast land. The strong visual statement that quilts made was national in scope and perhaps reinforced the patriotic cohesiveness that was binding an ever larger Union. Trends in the collection of patterns occurred in America's early days, just as fads ignite the design-conscious imagination today. Any interesting pattern or material would have been shared, while a natural spirit of competition probably stimulated many attempts to improve upon any new idea.

The combination of a single color with a white ground, for example, was a stylistic convention that developed as quilters expanded their repertoires beyond appliquéing fancy fabrics or piecing dark utility quilts. As Edward Binney and Gail Binney-Winslow note, "by working in one color on white, a quiltmaker was better able to refine, manipulate, and create designs, the distraction inherent in a multitude of printed fabrics or colors thus obliterated" (*Homage to Amanda*, 51). This led to advancements in the development of geometric patterns, from which optical illusions could naturally emerge.

Little formal training in the creation of patterns existed in the early years of the nation. Young women's education in handicrafts focused on needlework for the preparation of household articles and garments. Instruction covered music, literature, and etiquette, as well, but concentrated on the practical housekeeping skills. In the early academies or female schools to which girls of the upper classes were sent, art training was restricted to needlework or painting on paper or velvet. Students learned representational drawing of naturalistic forms—flowers, fruit, foliage, animals, people, and landscapes. Drawing manuals, prints, and engravings were their sources of design. The stenciling and découpage skills which might have inspired a creative quiltmaker to attempt transparent, layered effects did not occur until the second half of the nineteenth century.

Few women were able to obtain training in the arts or even to gain appreciation of the fine arts in colonial days; their education increased only as the nation expanded westward. According to Carrie Hall, "There were no schools of design open to our pioneer mothers; for the most part, the patterns were of quite simple geometric shapes, many of them having been used for generations" (*The Romance of the Patchwork Quilt in America*, 260). Moreover, there was little access for women to the basics of construction, mathematics, and geometry which young men would have needed to acquire as practical skills for their livelihood. But, "who shall say that woman's mind is inferior to man's, when, with little knowledge of mathematics, these women worked at geometric designs so intricate, and correlated each patch to all others in the block?" (ibid., 4).

A review of the indexes of books dealing with quilts and quiltmaking reveals, surprisingly, that few authors have established a category for optical effect, optical design, or illusion as a subject. Only Jonathan Holstein has analyzed the concept to any degree. He reviewed popular women's publications of the period 1830-1898, such as *Godey's Lady's Book*, and found only seventy-five published piecework patterns (among a multitude for crazy quilts and appliqué work). Of those patterns, only a handful were designed in the block style which had the greatest potential for variation. Other journals of the period were addressed mostly to rural audiences, barely mentioned quilts, and contained no patterns, Holstein concluded, since their audience was not the "middle class aspirant, but rather rural folks who made cotton and wool quilts strictly for warmth. The women who made functional quilts—and made up the patterns— were largely unschooled and certainly not trained in geometry. Yet they, and perhaps their husbands, had a practical knowledge of design which they used in their daily work" (*The Pieced Quilt*, 56).

Early authors researching old quilts were apt to be sentimental about them and were often unable to identify origins for the designs. Pioneer women may have written letters and kept diaries, but rarely described their creative processes in detail, reporting instead on the social interaction of quilting bees or their personal feelings about familial experiences. Books of the 1920s and '30s, with diagrammatic explanations of pattern construction, characterized earlier graphic quilts as "dramatic," "interesting," or "complicated to make," but gave few clues to the manipulation of pattern that led to some of the livelier examples featured here.

What, then, might have inspired quiltmakers to create designs of illu-

FIG. 2.2. Roman Square (Basketweave variation) pattern pieced quilt, c. 1925, Ohio. Maker unknown. 78″ x 69″. Cotton. Square blocks made of light and dark strips pieced in careful sequence to afford the greatest contrast have been alternated in direction across the quilt surface. The result of this arrangement is an illusion of three-dimensionality that resembles woven material as it might appear under a magnifying glass, or a network of woven ribbons. Because of the illusion of closure, the viewer mentally completes the linkage of the strong diagonals, even though these lines are interrupted by blocks facing in the opposite direction. (*Photo courtesy Darwin D. Bearley.*)

sion? There is a wealth of probable sources, ranging from elements in the natural environment to everyday household objects like textiles and woodwork, architectural ornamentation, tile work, and motifs in stone, metal, and wood from other cultures and ages. During the Victorian and Edwardian eras (1837-1910), cultural changes in England and the United States encouraged education in, and the application of, design, and revolutionary ideas in the fine arts fostered an environment that liberated creative expression.

Of course, a quilter needed to look no farther than her window, where light casting shadows, filtered by lace curtains or architectural ornaments, left a geometric image that could be translated into cloth. Natural objects like the growth rings of trees, the planes of a crystal geode, or the tracery of a snowflake could be equally suggestive. Patterns abounded in the landscape, modulated by light and ready for interpretation in fabric by a creative person.

Woven fabrics used for domestic textiles were also a ready source of

FIG. 2.3. Double cloth (double weave) geometric coverlet, c. 1840, probably Northeast. Maker unknown. 74″ x 64″. Wool and cotton. Durable bed-coverings of this type were composed of two separate layers of cloth which were con-nected in the weaving process to form the geometric motifs. Commonly, only two colors were used: an indigo blue for the dark (wool) component and a natural (cotton) for the light component which, woven together, provide the contrast. This particular coverlet is an unusual combination of three colors—red, black, and yellow. Professional weavers using multiple-shaft looms generally manufactured these more com-plex bedcovers: the simpler overshot coverlets and blankets were most commonly made at home. It was possible to achieve a considerable variety of weaving designs on even the simplest home looms. House-hold bedding and linens ap-pear in weaving patterns called twill, tabby, diaper, blanket, and damask variations, among others. Because most coverlets were set up schematically in blocks, and all incorporate an over-and-under formula to compose a design, their pat-terns were easy to emulate in quilt piecework. (*Author's collec-tion; photo by Peter W. Glasser.*)

geometric designs. For example, gingham checks have a warp of one col-or and a weft of another which cross over and under in sequence to create a third color. Madras plaids, originating in India and exported the world over for centuries, are composed of woven cotton threads in verti-cal and horizontal schemes that create mixed-color blocks. Tartan plaids and argyle checks, with their colorful backgrounds and strong geometric shapes, make easily translatable designs (fig. 3.56).

Weaving and basketry, both ancient arts, produced interlaced designs sugggesting depth. American coverlets, woven in two or more colors, developed intricate geometric designs that were precursors of some quilts

Fig. 2.4. Carpenter's Wheel (Broken Star variation) pattern pieced quilt, Mennonite, c. 1880, Lancaster County, Pennsylvania. Maker unknown. 76" square. Cotton. A great ribbon of pink and green undulates around a group of eight-pointed stars which seem to pop forward from this rich background because of the contrast of their scale to the overall graphic design. The single large-scale Carpenter's Wheel pattern is always associated with Lancaster County, Pennsylvania. Typically, it reads as flat and boldly colored, despite its angled edges. Here, the inclusion of tiny stars in the blocks between the central star and outlying pointed border adds spatial dimension that makes this pattern strikingly contemporary in its artistic impression. Ancient floor-tile patterns achieve a similar sense of undulating depth by incorporating various shades of marble or stone. (*Author's collection.*)

Fig. 2.5. Parquetry work, English and American, nineteenth century. Wood, shell, and/or papier maché. For several centuries, the surfaces of many household articles, small storage boxes, and furniture have been decorated with tiny pieces of wood, paper, or shell of various colors and geometric shapes. The most frequently encountered graphic design is some variation of the Tumbling Blocks pattern, but many three-dimensional geometric motifs associated with quiltmaking were executed in wood, stone, marble, and other materials long before they were translated to fabric. (*Author's collection; photo by Peter W. Glasser.*)

FIG. 2.6. Strip Star Maze pattern pieced quilt, c. 1875, probably Pennsylvania. Maker unknown. Dimensions unavailable. Cotton. This visual whirlwind actually has an orderly construction of fine narrow strips pieced first in diamond forms and then joined in an arrangement much like mosaic tile. The varying angles of the strips and the edges of the pattern elements draw the eye in, out, and around the composition, simultaneously veiling and revealing the star-like plan of the design. Such a turbulent effect most likely reflects the quiltmaker's need to use up precious scraps of fabric and her artistry in conquering the challenge of organizing the pieces. (*Photo courtesy Darwin D. Bearley.*)

of illusion (see figs. 2.3 and 3.77). The manufactured printed textiles which replaced handwoven goods by the nineteenth century were also inspirations for quilt patterns; simulated patchwork designs of great complexity and intricate scale could have been models for quiltmakers.

Probably the greatest sources for illusions, however, were found in architectural ornamentation and woodcraft. Ancient motifs from many cultures—Greek, Roman, Etruscan, early Christian, Middle Eastern, Islamic, Moorish, and Oriental—are echoed in quilt patterns. As early as the fifth century, B.C., glass mosaics and architectural ornaments in wood, stone, and metal evinced elements of design that were optical illusions. Some quilt patterns that appear multi-layered echo architectural support systems of webbed and balanced construction, stained-glass joinery techniques, or cloisonné or damascene metalwork, in their tracery designs.

In ancient Greece, Mesopotamia, Egypt, and the Orient, mathematical systems influenced the development of ornamental decoration. According to Stuart Durant, "Roman craftsmen were expert in setting out geometrical designs and were in possession of almost all the drawing instruments known to us, including compasses, proportional dividers, and set squares" (*Ornament*, 63). Some early mosaic designs were based on a grid of equilateral triangles combined to make an overall pattern of hexagons (figs. 3.81 and 3.114). Many of these designs were brought to Great Britain, where they reappeared in mosaic floors, in Celtic crosses, and in knot work.

The highest development of ornamental art based on geometry stems from the Islamic culture, where animal forms could not be represented in any artistic medium. As early as the thirteenth century, Islamic designs were emulated in European paving stones. Helen Fairfield has noticed the similarity of some quilt patterns to ancient Italian stone floors in Florence and Venice: "Some 400 years of effort, whose geometric designs stem from the eleventh through the fifteenth centuries, could have been designed for working in patchwork. With clever use of shape and shade, the paviors of Venice created intricate designs, many of which possess remarkable illusions of a third dimension" (*Patchwork from Mosaics*, 7).

Dozens of familiar quilt designs, including such patterns as the Le-Moyne Star (fig. 1.6), Carpenter's Wheel (fig. 1.14), Star of the East (fig. 2.1), and Baby's Blocks (fig. 3.54) can be traced to ancient tile work. Italian masters of mosaic migrated throughout Europe, introducing their designs to many other countries. Some quilts are assembled from a group of pre-formed parts set within sashing, much as ancient stained glass, cloisonné, or mosaic tesserae are set in a matrix of plaster or joined with a network of metal solder, iron bars, or stone tracery. This style of piecing visually links a grid which in many quilts appears to overlay other pattern elements. As in stained glass, a quilt image may seem to "continue" beneath the grid which separates the colored pieces from each other (figs. 3.10, 3.57, and 3.73).

The venerable art of woodcrafting may have inspired quilt designs. Elaborate parquetry inlays embellished fashionable tea caddies, writing boxes, case furniture, and decorative accessories which were brought to the United States from Europe. These pieced designs, showing depth through the use of different shades or types of wood inlay, frequently resemble Tumbling Blocks patterns (fig. 2.5).

Decorative furniture was carved, veneered, inlaid, or painted. Some painted furniture was made to convey the illusion of carving with *faux* modelled forms and incised lines to suggest depth. Those who could not afford inlay or marble could re-create the look through *trompe l'oeil* graining or marbleizing. Many early colonial polychrome chests show geometric elements akin to illusionary quilt designs, such as segmented circles representing the Tudor Rose that transposed realistic forms on a flat surface.

Increased consciousness about design that would have encouraged experimentation with quilt patterns flourished in the nineteenth century, as revolutions in the industrial and applied arts began to affect the creation of everyday objects. Scientists and laymen alike began to investigate the notion of what makes form. A scientific movement begun in the 1830s to study the "persistence of vision" led to the invention of devices to "capture" motion. This merging of magic and science captivated a widening lay audience. Experiments filtered down to many households in the form of paper ephemera and post cards that included images layered to produce depth. Optical toys of many varieties created movement from inertia and revealed hidden images. There was great interest in investigating the magical properties of the eye. The kaleidoscope, invented in 1817, transformed shapes through the use of lenses which distorted angles of

vision rather than changing the shape of the actual object. Other toys focused on the idea of anamorphic images, where a hidden form emerges from a relatively straightforward combination of designs.

Pattern books on optics, folding toys and cards that transformed images, and some highly sophisticated motion toys were popular and undoubtedly inspired creative people to explore optical phenomena in other media. Among the devices invented were magic lanterns; thaumatropes (where two images when spun merge as one); zoetropes, which convey an illusion of motion through a spinning drum mounted with different pictures; polyrama pyroptiques (home version dioramas); as well as the more familiar stereopticon and, later, the camera. Through all of these inventions, an awareness was undoubtedly fostered that two dimensions could be made to appear three-dimensional using perspective, distortion, and lenses or manipulated sources of light. As with these optical toys, quilts of illusion merge old images into new ones, create a suggestion of movement, and reveal that *what we get is not always what we see.*

Needleworkers began to imbue their quilts' flat surfaces with suggestions of a third dimension during the Victorian era, a time when concepts of design, works of art, and materials from other cultures were brought in great quantity and variety to a growing America. Because most antique quilts reflect the social climate in which they were made, an increasingly complex society was likely to have stimulated increasing intricacy in quilt design. The expansion of trade and travel educated

Americans to the art and culture of other places; people traveled more widely, and artists exchanged design ideas freely.

The concurrent Industrial Revolution transformed society, mechanizing handwork and spawning a variety of new designs. The corresponding emergence of a middle class, with newfound time and money which could be used to experiment with home furnishings, led to an increased awareness and acquisition of decorative objects. From the 1870s onward, books and journals on decoration of the household, including Charles Eastlake's *Hints on Household Taste* and Clarence Cook's *The House Beautiful,* proliferated. The everyday domestic environment of the emerging middle class contained endless sources of inspiration for the quilter. Wallpaper patterns, textiles, carpets, ceramics, metalwork, glass and china, advertising trade cards, painting and sculpture, and even book design contributed significantly to the design aesthetic of American quilts. Motifs from Middle Eastern, early European, and Oriental sources were commonplace. Patterning abounded; objects with strong graphic designs might be created of multiple layers of material. Japanese art, with its surface designs mostly flattened and stylized, exerted considerable influence.

During the design explorations of the aesthetic movement of the 1870's and '80s and the arts and crafts movement of the early 1900s, quiltmakers may have been exposed to the newly popular philosophies that anyone could create art and that everything could be made beautiful through the application of design. The concept of layering or juxtaposing different patterns was the hallmark of the aesthetic movement, whose principles of art filtered into all aspects of domestic life. The strong linear motifs of the movement inspired a stylized, geometrized flattening of forms which dominated ideas and design and could be found in goods manufactured at the end of the nineteenth century. In addition, women were beginning to gain increased acceptance as professional artists, applying these philosophies of design to needlework, ceramics, and textiles. Art, and formal education in art, became important; consciousness about design was rampant. As interior design became a recognized profession, American homes were illustrated in journals that exposed their lavish detailing for all to copy. National schools of design were opened; art clubs and art schools that taught more than needleworking skills were established.

Stuart Durant reports that, from the 1880s onward, the making of pattern was actually taught in manuals which showed how repeat patterns could be constructed using grids (*Ornament*, 73). Instructive toys were invented, among them the Froebel architectural stone blocks said to have inspired Frank Lloyd Wright, and other mosaic amusements featuring small bits of wood or tile which allowed children to experiment with geometric form (fig. 2.7).

In 1880, Frederick Ad. Richter and Company, the foremost manufacturer of pattern-making toys, construction blocks, and puzzles, produced a mosaic set with plans to create patterned floors and walls. Such toys actively involved children in design. Even machines for drawing patterns, such as the "epicycloidal geometric chuck" (1910), which might have been used to design quilt patterns as well as home interiors, were developed (ibid., 75). During the Victorian era, an age in which the family unit was inviolable, children were included in many household projects, including that of quiltmaking. They began early in life, had ample free time, and reaped the benefit of new educational methods of training which encouraged experimentation.

From the mid-nineteenth century onward, radical innovations in the art of painting seem to parallel the increasing experimentation in quilt design. The impressionists, whose work was first exhibited in the United

FIG. 2.9. Workbook of interwoven and folded designs, dated September 21, 1888, locale unknown. Made by Edith L. Aldrich. Paper. This fascinating workbook/scrapbook contains handmade plates that are exercises in geometric design. Some have been folded, as in Japanese origami, others are composed of interwoven shiny paper cut into strips. Different graphic effects have been created by varying the sequence of strips in the interlacing. (*Author's collection; photo by Peter W. Glasser.*)

States in 1886, investigated the representation of light on canvas. Seurat and other post-impressionists were interested in the science of optics: through their technique of pointillism, dots of separate color, when seen from a distance, merge into solid objects. In subsequent art movements like cubism, surrealism, and abstract expressionism, painters began to treat their subjects in new ways. Surfaces became flattened and images broken into stylized planes. Artists like Bracque, Picabia, Duchamp, and Picasso created geometric abstractions. Experimentation flourished on both sides of the Atlantic, reaching a zenith in the creations of the Wiener Werkstätte, whose principal designer, Koloman Moser, produced textiles of reversible imagery that resemble some of the quilt patterns featured here (figs. 3.105 and 3.115). At the same time, American quilters were achieving parallel innovations in design, for a spirit of experimentation was in the air.

During the 1920s and '30s, modernistic designs were found stamped on every kind of domestic product from pressed-glass dinnerware and icebox doors to the packaging of laundry soap. Such motifs were omnipresent, and quilters were likely to have been influenced by the streamlined environment around them, whether or not they were aware of the radical changes taking place in the art world.

M.C. Escher (1898-1972) is perhaps the principal artist whose name evokes images of optical illusion in design. This Dutch painter created illusionary volumes of shifting perspectives on flat surfaces in such designs as metamorphoses, cycles, and approaches to infinity, designs which are also seen in some of the quilts featured here (figs. 1.22 and 3.2). There are strong similarities between Escher's work and that of quilt designers working in the same period (the 1920s and '30s), as there are between mid-twentieth-century movements such as op art and pop art and much earlier quilts. As Jean Lipman suggests, op art painters, who created large-scale geometric abstractions by juxtaposing bold colors for dramatic effect, may have been inspired by quilts conceived as much as a century earlier (*Provocative Parallels,* 117). For example, while contemporary artist Ellsworth Kelly may carefully plan the color harmony and contrast inherent in his paintings, nineteenth- and early twentieth-century quilters are felt to have had an intuitive sense of color that produced much the same result long before Kelly was born.

Perhaps some makers of quilts of illusion did not look at all to the outside world for inspiration, but came to their remarkable graphic designs motivated solely by some inner vision and personal creative genius that needed no external confirmation. After all, it was an indomitable group of pioneers and adventurers who conquered the American West. The hardships they faced and the ingenuity needed to overcome them might have found expression in complex quilt patterns that transform a seeming chaos into order. The truly creative quiltmaker always tried something different, rather than going along with the crowd. Someone without that creative inspiration would make a serviceable but unremarkable quilt, while the same patches organized by special hands and minds achieved artistic brilliance.

3.
QUILTS OF ILLUSION: A PORT-FOLIO

O A MODERN ART LOVER, the following portfolio may suggest the works of such artists as Frank Stella, Victor Vasarely, Richard Anuszkiewicz, Georges Bracque, Francis Picabia, Kolomon Moser, and other twentieth-century painters, rather than an album of quilts of illusion. And at first glance, quilt admirers accustomed to seeing elaborate flowers or eagles as representative of their favorite art form may not be able to appreciate these intricate, shifting patterns. But on further examination, the complex, mysterious, and dramatic qualities of these stunning quilts will emerge.

Ask a group of quilt aficionados to name an optical illusion pattern and almost unanimously the answer will be "Tumbling Blocks." Yet there are many other patterns that create optical illusions, including great series of Log Cabin variations, Stars, Bow Ties, Roman Stripes, and even Double Wedding Rings and floral appliqués. Probably any traditional geometric design, and the familiarly shaped elements within it, can be grouped and modified to generate striking graphic, illusionary results. Readers who think they "know" the Tumbling or Baby Blocks pattern may be surprised to see the optical tricks those cubes can play.

The pieced (and infrequently, appliqué) quilts that follow generally have an overall geometric design which is based on the repetition of a single element or pattern block. The colors chosen and the juxtaposition of pieces within the total framework of the design have led to some remarkable optical effects. Although their first role was to serve as ordinary and useful household objects, these patchworks have become visually engaging works of art in the hands of imaginative quilters. While hard-pressed pioneer women had little time to consider decorating their rustic log cabins with works of art, their subconscious needs for self expression were met in some measure in their quilting. The more talent a seamstress possessed, the more complicated her designs were likely to be.

The quiltmaker of illusions may have had an innate facility for, or understanding of, mathematical or geometric concepts to guide her design, but more than likely the most disarming of the optical effects occurred spontaneously because of the unpredictable interactions of cloth and color and line. Many of the examples of the quilter's art included here are akin to geometric forms such as the tetrahedron, the hexahedron, and so on, but few quiltmakers are likely to have had training in geometry to the degree that would have directed the creation of patterns. Although most blocks comprising the overall quilt surface are assumed to have been planned beforehand, some of the powerful results shown here undoubtedly astonished their makers with unanticipated dimensions of movement and depth.

In all of the examples which follow, the visual "whole" is greater than the sum of its actual parts—seemingly impossible in reality, but a magical by-product of the quiltmaker's artistry.

Any quiltmaker, anywhere, could create an optical illusion quilt. Examples have surfaced in all parts of the United States and cannot be attributed to any particular region or group (unlike antique Broderie Perse quilts, for example, which stem from the original Thirteen Colo-

FIG. 3.1. Kaleidoscope pattern pieced quilt, fabrics c. 1930, made in 1974, Chattanooga, Tennessee. Made by Bets Ramsey. 84" x 70". Cotton. This is one of the few instances in pattern nomenclature where the name conveys the image. An eye-dazzling composition of circles and triangles seems to spin and twist in constant motion. Simultaneously, the viewer perceives concave four-pointed stars, small dark circles composed of wedge-shaped triangular segments, and illuminated disks that seem to overlay the surface's kinetic underpinnings. Because each pattern piece is shared by neighboring designs, an illusion of interrupted systems conveys the impression of transparency as some areas veil other aspects of the overall design. (Collection of Bets Ramsey. Photo courtesy Quilts of Tennessee.)

nies, or Baltimore Album quilts, which originated at a certain period of time in a particular place). Interestingly, many of the best examples come from Amish communities, where a tradition of sensitivity to color in its purest form, without the distraction of pattern, led to an eloquent expression of design. Certainly twentieth-century color-field artists and theorists like Josef Albers could look to these Amish illusions to study the interaction of color. It is ironic that the Amish produced so many examples of illusionary quilts, because in the earliest, most orthodox settlements, some sect leaders forbade the piecing of quilts. Interaction with their non-Amish neighbors introduced these simple people to American quilting traditions which, coupled with their indigenous color sensibility, led to the creation of truly radiant graphic masterpieces.

Any seamstress, whether Amish or not, probably began a new quilt with a basic form in mind and let her creative instincts motivate the preparation and assembly of her pieces. By experimenting, she could explore possible patterns from scraps without having to compose an entire design. Or she might have created a pattern using graph paper or paper templates folded in equal parts upon which different colors or design elements could be drawn to explore combinations for their effects. After deciding on her overall design, the quiltmaker might have created her own patterns from paper, pressboard, or other stiff template; marked the patches; figured out the amount of material required for the different components; and begun to sew.

This portfolio of quilts is organized according to the predominant geometric forms that comprise the blocks or pattern segments, just as the quiltmaker would have approached her project. The *basis* for the illusion is our starting point, as the geometric forms employed are the piecing elements most familiar to quilt lovers and quiltmakers alike: the square and the triangle; the diamond and the cube; the rectangle and the strip; curvilinear forms, including circles and hexagons; and, finally, combinations of representational, eccentric, miscellaneous, and unique patterns. The three basic geometric designs in earliest use in American patchwork quilting were the square, the rectangle, and the diamond. The circle and hexagon were considered secondary to these three basic forms. Together, these five geometric shapes, and the parts into which each can be easily subdivided, constitute the piecework vocabulary for the majority of quilts.

To demonstrate how the use of different tonal combinations and relative size can alter a traditional pattern, this chapter includes several examples of each of the more familiar quilt patterns, such as Baby Blocks, Stars, Log Cabins, and block work. In conjunction with the many illustrations depicting the full quilts, details are included to highlight interesting aspects of the designs. Some examples are one of a kind, taking off perhaps from a familiar concept, but modifying it in a highly original and sometimes explosive way.

Many of the examples included here have no recorded pattern names. The titles that accompany them either stem from the geometric format of the design closest to a traditional example, or are affectionate or picturesque descriptions which the owners have given them. Most pattern names were derived from historic, geographic, botanical, political, socio-cultural, religious, or familial sources. While the names are charming, they usually give no hint as to the formal composition of the block or the finished quilt. For example, quilts with the word "puzzle" in their name may have been so called because they contain a number of differently shaped geometric pieces. Or designs like Yankee Puzzle, Irish Puzzle, Chinese Puzzle, and others might have emerged at a time of mass emigration to the United States and have little to do with design complexity. The "puzzle" design closest to a real illusion is Tile Puzzle, whose frame of reference is the intricately webbed ancient Islamic patterning which seems to have influenced many of the quilts included here (see fig. 3.116).

Each illustration in this portfolio is accompanied by a legend which follows a basic format. First is noted the pattern name as recorded in a published source or submitted by the maker, family of the maker, or current owner. Next is the date, either preceded by "c." if estimated, or as recorded by the original source. Then the materials used to piece the top are cited, with the primary fabric listed first. Any regional or historical information, including the maker's name, has been included when known. When measurements are available, length precedes width. A description of the basic building blocks of the overall design follows, with some analysis of how the graphic effects are perceived.

Few legends contain information on family provenance, for most have been acquired through a network that dislocated them from their family of origin and any anecdotal material that might have shed light on how these designs came into being. After all, these quilts are prized for their artistic attributes, their graphic appeal, and their mastery of design. All too frequently, the social context which might have illuminated their creation has been obliterated by time.

Squares and Triangles

THE SQUARE, perhaps the most commonly used geometric shape in quiltmaking, is a rectangle with four equal sides. This basic unit of block design is the source for the term "block work," for the earliest known American pieced quilts incorporated some combination of square blocks. These could be employed to frame a central square with outer borders, as in the central medallion format, or be formed of scraps, creating a pleasing foundation from which to build a design. Patches could also be sewn into a square block which was treated as a single unit for purposes of larger composition.

This most basic unit of quilt-block composition can be easily cut and simply varied in scale or coloration to build a successful quilt design. Some variation of the square—the right-angle triangle, created by bisecting the square in half diagonally, or the rectangle, by bisecting it in half vertically—constitutes the basis for innumerable quilt patterns. The quiltmaker using triangles has the option of keeping some pairs in the same color and varying the colors of others to create a pattern using simple pieces. She does not need a template, other than the pattern for the square, to create triangles: they can be cut by folding the square on the diagonal and clipping it.

Compositions employing the repetition of one patch of identical size rely on variations of shading and color rather than form for their graphic effect. Other

FIG. 3.2. Diamond in a Square to Infinity (One-Patch variation) pattern pieced quilt, c. 1925, Muncie, Indiana. Maker unknown. 84″ square. Cotton and rayon. Some 15,000 postage-stamp-sized pieces have been organized by color and shading to produce an extraordinary large-scale abstraction that conveys near and deep space simultaneously. At the center, subtly shaded pastels create small diamonds in squares, which appear to be laid on top of each other until they confront rust-colored perimeters. As the eye tries to decipher this microscopic activity, it is at the same time distracted by the quilt's corners, where deeply hued layers appear as if peeled back to reveal underlying layers. The pieces have been sewn edge to edge in the standard fashion, but the illusion is one of several planes of fabric. Around the time this quilt was executed, many national competitions were held with prizes given to quilts made using the greatest number of pieces; this one surely approaches a record and was generations ahead of its time in its sweeping, painterly treatment of its images. (*First published in* The Quilt Digest 5; *photo courtesy The Quilt Digest Press.*)

FIG. 3.3. Double Nine-Patch pattern pieced quilt, Amish, c. 1920, Ohio. Maker unknown. 79″ x 70″. Cotton. What at first glance appears to be a sampler quilt of twenty blocks separated by dark sashing is actually a group of identical nine-patch blocks which read differently depending on their color juxtaposition and relative intensity. In some blocks, a diagonal crisscross dominates; in others, the small solid squares "pop" to read as solid crosses, when actually they serve only to separate the smaller pieced patches; others look like solid checkerboards as their color differences merge; and in still others the small patches appear to float free. The blocks were probably made of scraps without any effort to coordinate the colors into a visual whole across the quilt surface. It's fun to examine each block to discover further variations that color produces (*Photo courtesy Darwin D. Bearley.*)

multiple square patterns, using patches of different scale and color, tend to be grouped in larger squares, composed usually of four or nine patches, and set within a grid or framework to organize the design.

Examples given here range from illusions which include a few dozen squares of limited color variation where strategic placement of colors forms a pattern, such as Double Nine-Patch (fig. 3.3), to examples where thousands of pieces have been carefully coordinated to achieve the effect (fig. 3.2).

Squares are easy to multiply to form different designs. Probably at least half of all known pieced quilt patterns are formulated on some multiple of the square, with most assuming the four-patch or nine-patch configuration. In these, alternating the color in a regular fashion creates a visible, larger-scale, pattern.

The Bow Tie pattern and its variations are actually a version of a nine-patch pattern. In this grouping of nine squares, eight have their inner corners clipped diagonally to allow the inclusion of a small square at the center of the group. Bow Tie blocks are arranged most often with the center square and the upper and lower opposing patches cut from the same color fabric in order to display the bow tie configuration. Each pattern block of nine squares can be colored and rotated in relation to its neighboring blocks in ways that create a great variety of graphic quilt patterns. In some more dramatic examples included here, the viewer must search to locate the bow tie within the optical presentation. Among the Amish, with their particular color sensibility, the Bow Tie pattern achieved an intensity of exaggerated image—even though the use of bow ties by Amish men was eschewed as unnecessary adornment!

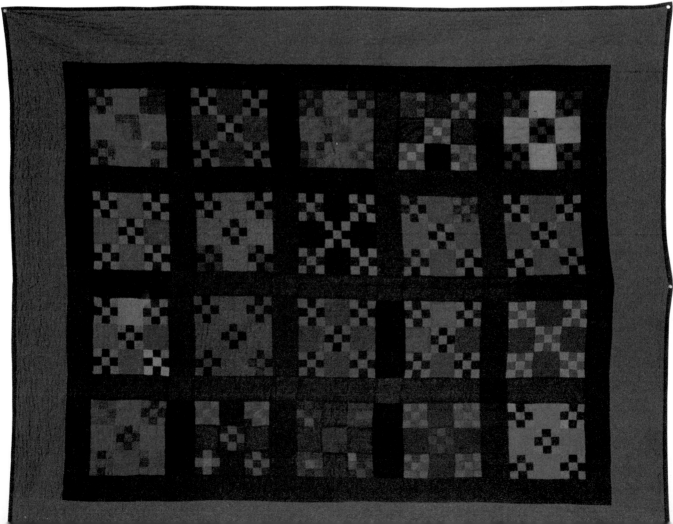

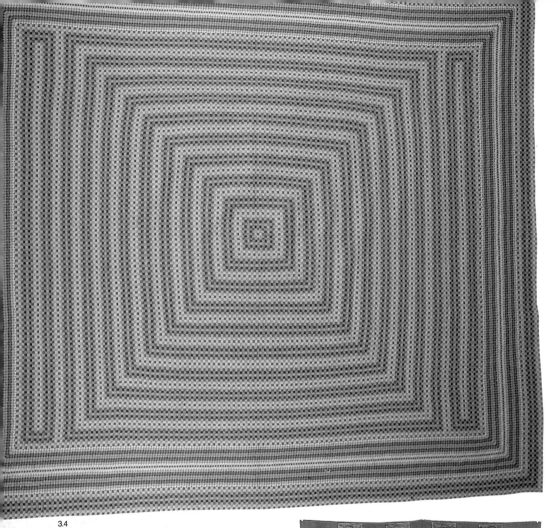

3.4

of a maze. This same sense of endless space conveyed by increasing or diminishing elements is expressed in figure 1.12. The illusion achieved masterpiece status in the hands of George Yarrall, a jewelry engraver reported to have taken up quilting to keep his hands limber. He began the quilt on July 2, 1933, and finished it on December 30, 1935, arranging ten colors of percale into a series of borders, panels, and a center to present an enigmatic vortex. (*Photo courtesy The Kentucky Museum, Western Kentucky University.*)

FIG. 3.5. Coarse Woven (One-Patch variation) pattern pieced quilt, c. 1910, locale unknown. Maker unknown. 79″ x 69″. Cotton. Gradient patterning creates an illusion of three dimensionality in this simply constructed One-Patch variation. Peaks and valleys outlined in dark shades appear as if in constant motion above a light ground. At the same time, the zigzags appear to bleed into the white areas and prevent the eye from focusing, thanks to the quilter's skillful shading of the zigzags in lighter tones. This pattern is also called Flamestitch or Fine Woven, inspired probably by needlework which is done in a continual up-and-down, in-and-out motion, rather than the contiguous piecing method by which a quilt is usually constructed. (*Photo courtesy Darwin D. Bearley.*)

FIG. 3.6. Hit-or-Miss pattern pieced quilt, c. 1920, locale unknown. Maker unknown. 79″ x 64″. Cotton. By imaginatively moving each rectangle of identical color one half length down, the quilter produces a dramatic graphic, which fools the viewer into thinking that the quilt has sagged in the middle, or that a thread has been pulled which distorts the quilt surface. A simple rectangular form in two primary colors is employed in a striking and unconventional manner with whimsical result. Where another maker might have aligned the ingots in rows like a Bars pattern, or in alternation like a checkerboard, this quilt's creator moves the image into the realm of the abstract through her employment of a novel geometric configuration. (*Photo courtesy Darwin D. Bearley.*)

3.5

3.6

FIG. 3.4. Spectrum (One-Patch variation) pattern pieced quilt, c. 1935, Bowling Green, Kentucky. Made by George W. Yarrall. 90¾″ x 78½″. Cotton percale. A composition which appears to be concentric squares made of strips is actually constructed of 66,153 pieces, each no longer than ¼″ or ⅜″. Their arrangement by shade within consecutive-length strips draws the viewer's attention into and out

Fig. 3.7. One-Patch Star pattern pieced quilt, Amish, c. 1930, possibly Midwest or Canada. Maker unknown. 80" x 72". Cotton. In this unusual Amish quilt, the elemental one patch has been organized by color to illuminate a brilliant star, atop a dark field, that seems to be pinned to the surface by a Diamond in the Square pattern. This unusual device gives the illusion of several layers of design. The dark and light contrasts also heighten the effect of pattern suspended above surface in the corners, where miniature Sunshine and Shadow graphics create additional visual trickery. (*Author's collection.*)

Fig. 3.8. Sunshine and Shadow (everted variation) pattern pieced quilt, Amish, c. 1915, Mifflin County, Pennsylvania. Maker unknown. 84" x 75". Wool and cotton. Look what can happen when a classic pattern is split down the middle and put together back to back. X marks the point of intersection with powerful optical effect. Because of the placement of related or contrasting shades, the X appears to be both chiseled into and beveled above the quilt surface. The use of a light outline underscores the three-dimensional effect. Through a trick of the eye, the four sides appear to be inching in toward the quilt's center, following imaginary lines that bisect the design vertically and horizontally. (*Photo courtesy Darwin D. Bearley.*)

Fig. 3.9. Double Nine-Patch pattern pieced quilt, Amish, c. 1930, Mifflin County, Pennsylvania. Maker unknown. Dimensions unavailable. Cotton sateen. The device of setting a pieced block on point adds variety to country quilts, and in the hands of a quilt artist can produce wonderful optical effects. Here, a multi-level, spatial illusion occurs from the linkages perceived both above and below the quilt's actual plane. A light horizontal and vertical grid has been created where the tiny nine-patch blocks join visually. This grid communicates a visual tension as it attempts to hold in check the wide, dark diagonal grid, which is actually the sashing separating the pieced blocks. (*Photo courtesy Judi Boisson Antique American Quilts.*)

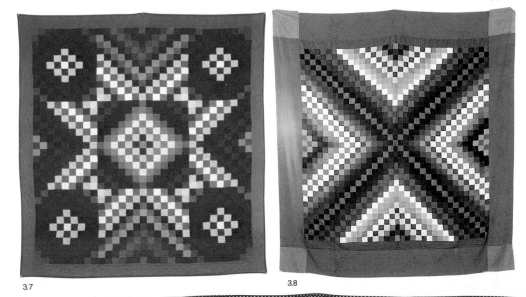

3.7   3.8

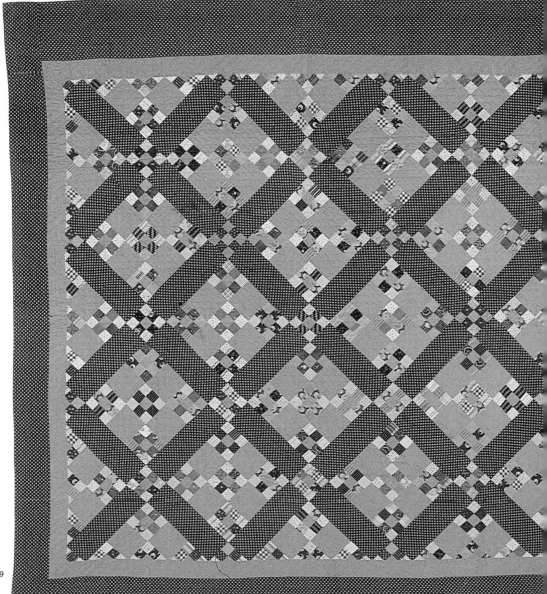

3.9

3.10

3.11

FIG. 3.10. Four-in-Nine-Patch pattern pieced quilt, Amish, c. 1920, Mifflin County, Pennsylvania. Maker unknown. 80″ x 71″. Cotton sateen. Multiple planes of pattern appear simultaneously in a complex design built from the simplest of geometric elements—the square block or patch. Each larger block includes both the four-patch and nine-patch elements which the Amish traditionally incorporated in their quilts. Here, these groupings have been set on point so that when they touch neighboring blocks the smaller squares within link up like pastel light strings in a horizontal and vertical grid above the quilt surface. That grid seems to overlay a complex spatial illusion: the olive-green sashing that frames the four-in-nine-patch blocks looks instead like a subordinate lattice-work grid beneath the patterned layers. The solid squares that separate the four-patch segments in each large block seem to merge in yet a third layer of pattern—dark crisscrosses connected beneath the olive grid. (*Photo courtesy Judi Boisson Antique American Quilts.*)

FIG. 3.11. Bow Tie (Floating Octagons variation) pattern pieced quilt, Amish, c. 1930, Ohio. Maker unknown. 45″ x 30″. Cotton. This small-scale example captures the exciting illusory qualities which the Bow Tie pattern can generate in skillful hands. Here, each little square block contains a pastel bow tie all of one color with green segments at the remaining two corners. Groups of four such squares have been arranged with the bow ties facing diagonally at each corner. As a result, a larger scale, actively patterned surface has been created, appearing simultaneously as if holes have been punched out to reveal green beneath, or as if octagons are floating above the surface. (*Photo courtesy Darwin D. Bearley.*)

FIG. 3.12. Bow Tie pattern pieced quilt detail, c. 1880, Massachusetts. Maker unknown. 100″ square. Wool challis, silk, and cotton. This detail is included for comparison with other Bow Tie examples to show how the quilter's decision not to organize the light and dark tones of the patches has led to the absence of any clear Bow Tie design. If the Bow Tie pattern is to produce optical tricks, tonal contrasts, rather than the shapes of the pieces, must be carefully orchestrated. The entire composition contains nearly 4,000 clipped square patches of patterned Victorian fabrics, giving it an intricate, rich appearance. Yet the surface has little illusion of depth or movement except in the rare areas where some of the fabric tones have been accidentally aligned. (*Author's collection.*)

FIG. 3.13. Bow Tie pattern pieced quilt. Amish, c. 1930, Ohio. Maker unknown. 78″ x 70″. Cotton. Diagonal bands of the bow tie squares assume a variety of shapes because of the fanciful combination of intense lights and darks. The lightest shades seem to generate the most distinct bow ties. In areas where the bow ties are dark, and more closely related in hue to their neighbors, such images as octagons, butterfly hinges, and checkerboard blocks emerge. No one image dominates because there is so much movement conveyed by the consistency of shades on the diagonals that course up the quilt surface. (*Photo courtesy Darwin D. Bearley.*)

3.12

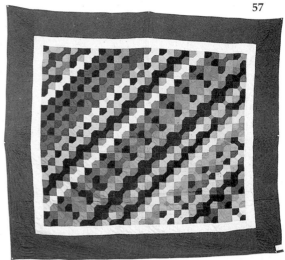
3.13

FIG. 3.14. One-Patch Diamond in a Square pattern pieced quilt, Amish, c. 1930, Midwest. Maker unknown. 80″ square. Rayon gabardine. By rotating the direction of a chief visual element and outlining it, the quiltmaker has visually suggested that there are two separate layers of pattern, which we know that technically there are not. Here is another example of how with a little imagination the most basic element of patchwork—the square block—can be transformed into a strikingly modern visual abstraction. (*Author's collection.*)

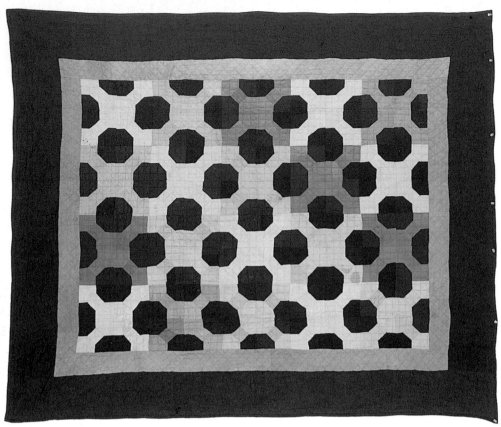

FIG. 3.15. Bow Tie (Octagonal variation) pattern pieced quilt, Amish, c. 1900, Iowa. Maker unknown. Dimensions unavailable. Cotton. In this infrequently attempted variation, two Bow Tie blocks are shifted in their diagonal direction so as to create bold black octagons at the central meeting point of each group of four bow tie squares. In such examples, the octagons appear to float above the quilt surface as if they have been applied on a backdrop. That background's visual interest is further enhanced by the consistent organization of light tones on the diagonal. (*Photo courtesy Judi Boisson Antique American Quilts.*)

FIG. 3.16. Checkerboard (Bow Tie variation) pattern pieced quilt, Amish, c. 1930, Ohio. Maker unknown. 74" x 68". Cotton. An entirely different visual effect from other examples of this pattern has been achieved by restricting the palette of the familiar bow-tie composition to just two contrasting shades. The bow-tie structural elements have become completely sublimated to the checkerboard. Its alternating squares shift in the viewer's perception from the appearance of light octagons afloat on a dark ground to a dark grid laid over a lighter ground. (*Author's collection.*)

FIG. 3.17. Diagonal Triangles pattern pieced quilt, Amish, c. 1920, Holmes County, Ohio. Maker unknown. Dimensions unavailable. Cotton. Which triangles point the direction in which to read this quilt design—the dark or the light ones? Each half of this quilt, which is bisected on the diagonal by a pale strip, incorporates hundreds of triangles in diminishing rows which seem constantly to switch direction. Their sawtooth edges communicate a dynamic quality that activates the quilt surface. (*Photo courtesy Judi Boisson Antique American Quilts.*)

FIG. 3.18. Streak of Lightning (Roman Stripe variation) pattern pieced quilt, Amish, c. 1934, Topeka, LaGrange County, Indiana. Made by Susie Miller. 84″ x 82″. Wool and cotton. The Roman Stripe pattern in its simplest form is composed of squares, each of which is made up of two equilateral triangles, one in a solid fabric, the other composed of many fabric strips. This example is perhaps the boldest illusionist variation of the Roman Stripe patterns included here. The design has been composed in the usual way, by piecing square blocks half of solid triangles and half of multi-shaded strips. Although the strips' tones have not been coordinated, the whole reads as zigzags aligned so as to convey a sense of wavy movement, a mobile flow that occurs because of the persistence of vision phenomenon. (*Photo courtesy Esprit Quilt Collection.*)

FIG. 3.19. Ocean Waves pattern pieced quilt, Amish, c. 1915, Ohio. Maker unknown. 84″ x 79″. Cotton. Black diamonds appear to have fallen in a symmetrical pattern atop a turbulent background that looks like printed fabric, instead of the hundreds of richly hued pastel triangles of which it is pieced. The triangular piecework, which is characteristic of the pattern, is so dense here that it seems to merge visually as a solid field on which snippets of black float. The strongly optical effect of light and dark contrast is greater at the center than at the sides, where the gray, rather than black, diamonds are closer in value to their surroundings and thus exhibit less visual tension. (*Photo courtesy Darwin D. Bearley.*)

FIG. 3.20. Path Through the Woods pattern pieced quilt, c. 1890, Pennsylvania. Maker unknown. 83″ square. Cotton. Identically sized triangles of intricately patterned Victorian cottons have been coordinated by light and dark tones to produce concentric outlined squares that seem to expand from the quilt's center Broken Dishes square. While occasional deviations from this orchestrated harmony of tone occur, they fail to break the rhythm of the concentric pieced squares. In some areas, where the tone of contiguous triangles is related, shadowy diamonds appear to float up optically to capture the viewer's attention. (*Author's collection.*)

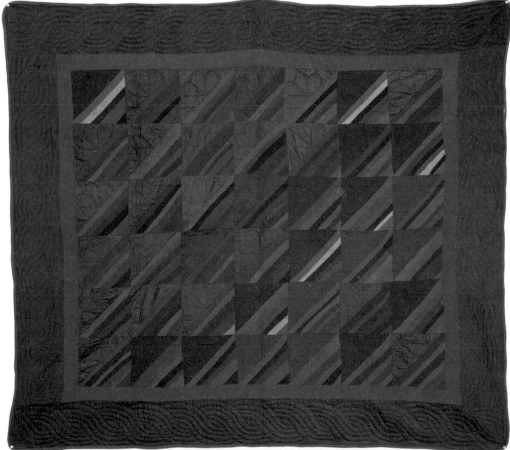

FIG. 3.21. Roman Stripe pattern pieced quilt, Amish, c. 1905, Holmes County, Ohio. Maker unknown. 78″ x 74″. Cotton and wool. This densely packed variation of a triangle-based pattern looks as if it was produced by three-dimensional computer wizardry. This modern, intergalactic landscape image is, surprisingly, a favorite pattern among the Amish, whose lifestyle and beliefs are very different from its contemporary style. The solid triangles, for which many different blacks were used, read as black or charcoal, matte or shiny, highly raised from the quilt surface or disappearing into the striped bands, because they react differently to the light source. Within this straightforward composition, there is much visual variety caused by light and color. The viewer cannot encompass the whole because a study of the parts reveals such differences. (*Photo courtesy Darwin D. Bearley.*)

3.22

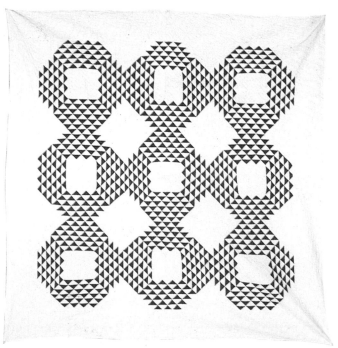

3.23

FIG. 3.22. Railroad Crossing pattern pieced quilt, Amish, c. 1935, Ohio. Maker unknown. Dimensions unavailable. Cotton. Patterns like this express an idea through abstraction rather than realism. The geometrics here direct the eye everywhere at once. Bold black solids appear as a grid placed over the subordinate beehive of activity conveyed by tiny solid-colored triangles, when in actuality these areas are one flat surface created by sewing patches together. The grid also recedes as the triangular areas merge as "town squares" in the viewer's perception through the phenomenon of closure, in which the eye perceives filled spaces that don't really exist. (*Photo courtesy Esprit Quilt Collection.*)

FIG. 3.23. Ocean Waves pattern pieced quilt, c. 1900, locale unknown. Maker unknown. 80″ square. Cotton. This crisp and dramatic graphic design seems to be two different things at once: light squares and diamonds laid on top of a patterned ground, and patterned fabric from which those geometric shapes have been cut out. By restricting the piecing to two fabrics (red and white), the powerful effect of the pattern has been heightened and emboldened. (*Photo courtesy Darwin D. Bearley.*)

Fig. 3. 24. Pinwheel pattern pieced quilt, c. 1920, locale unknown. Maker unknown. 75″ square. Cotton. A diagonal grid of miniature dark and white pinwheels seems to dance above and below a larger scale pinwheel ground. This illusion is caused in part by the effect of white pieces against white, which makes the grid seem at times like the absence of pattern. Its small scale in relation to other elements of the design also exaggerates the multi-level visual confusion and activity of the quilt surface. (*Photo courtesy Darwin D. Bearley.*)

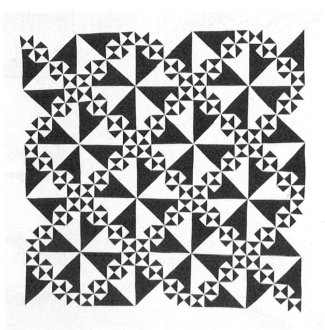

3.24

Fig. 3.25. Kansas Dugout (Roman Stripe variation) pattern pieced quilt, Amish, c. 1925, Ohio. Maker unknown. 87″ x 66″. Cotton. The same basic block used for figure 3.18 here has been worked in groups of four, with the striped and solid areas abutting each other, rather than being aligned in rows. Although no effort was made to correlate the sequence of strips so that the matching fabrics align when the blocks are joined, the eye perceives concentric diamonds folding out from their centers. The striped diamonds appear to be reflected in a mirror; although their image is broken, we "know" the other half is there. In addition, the solid areas of fabric compete equally as a design element for the viewer's attention. (*Photo courtesy Esprit Quilt Collection.*)

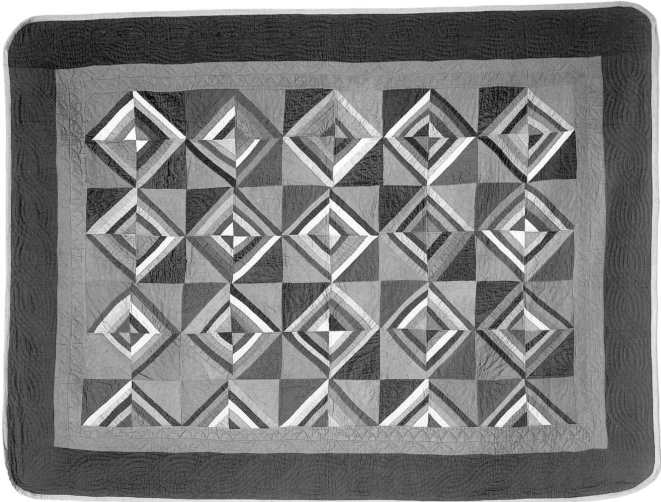

3.25

FIG. 3.26. Hayes' Corner pattern pieced quilt, Amish, c. 1930, Holmes County, Ohio. Maker unknown. 74" square. Cotton. The intense tonal contrasts of the diamond forms nearly dissolve the overlying stepped grid that is a hallmark of this infrequently executed pattern. In contrast to the other examples of the Hayes' Corner pattern included (figs. 3.45 and 3.120), here the concentric diamonds seem submerged beneath a light-toned veil, rather than floating on top. The closely related tonal values of the pattern pieces continually deceive as to which geometric form is dominant on the visual field. (*Author's collection.*)

FIG. 3.27. Ocean Waves pattern pieced quilt, Amish, c. 1930, Ohio. Maker unknown. Dimensions unavailable. Cotton. The solid centers of this intricate pattern seem to be surmounted by a highly sculpted, almost three-dimensional grid. It reminds the viewer of tramp art, where wood is chip carved and placed in increasingly smaller layers atop each other. Hundreds of tiny triangles suggest that wood effect and seem to raise the grid toward the viewer. In other Ocean Wave examples, the pieced triangles read more frequently as a printed fabric background. (*Photo courtesy Judi Boisson Antique American Quilts.*)

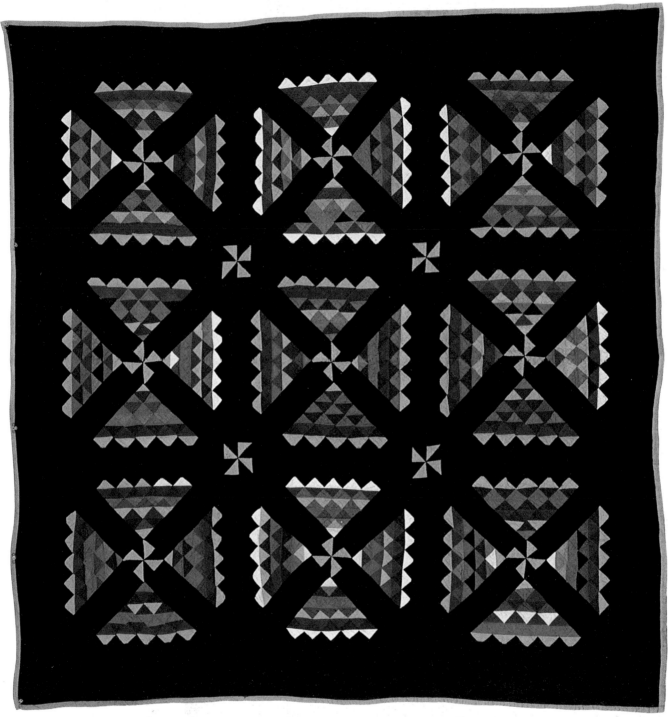

FIG. 3.28. Railroad Crossing pattern pieced quilt, Amish, c. 1915, Holmes County, Ohio. Maker unknown. Dimensions unavailable. Cotton. The black "tracks" converge in an iron-like diagonal and square grid visually raised above nine blocks of concentric sawtooth squares. The quiltmaker carefully orchestrated her sawtooth strips of tiny mauve, pink, rose, and blue triangles so they would read in successive outline as a further illusion. The eye is led in many directions at once from this design, traveling around the grids and pausing at the pink pinwheel intersections before taking off on another route. The black grid appears to have been laid down as a separate section, rather than joined contiguously to the triangular pieces. Railroad Crossing is one of the rarest Amish patterns. (*Photo courtesy Judi Boisson Antique American Quilts.*)

FIG. 3.29. Kaleidoscope pattern pieced quilt detail, fabrics c. 1930, finished in 1974, Chattanooga, Tennessee. Made by Bets Ramsey. 84" x 70". Cotton. As this detail reveals, complex piecing and tonal coordination produce the illusion of transparent overlays and geometric designs of stars, octagons, and propellers in this richly textured country quilt. A variety of patterned fabrics have been strategically laid out with attention to lights and darks to create an intriguing surface which seems to roll over itself as the eye follows the diagonal and curved edges. (*Collection of Bets Ramsey; photo courtesy Quilts of Tennessee.*)

FIG. 3.30. Delectable Mountains pattern pieced quilt, c. 1925, Ohio. Maker unknown. 75" square. Cotton. This uncommon variation of the Delectable Mountains pattern incorporates large triangles pieced of small pastel print squares to create the "mountains." Although the mountains are traditionally composed of triangles, the illusionary effect achieved here is the same. The quilt appears to be made of successive layers of squares laid on top of each other in decreasing size, but actually it is composed by the quilter adding one triangular element to each row as she moves outward from the center. The viewer imagines the mountain range expanding beyond the borders of the quilt. (*Photo courtesy Darwin D. Bearley.*)

FIGS. 3.31, 3.32. Pyramids (Triangles variation) pattern pieced quilt and detail, c. 1860, England. Maker unknown. 40″ x 34″. Silk. This luminescent crib quilt or parlor throw, composed of one-inch triangles, illustrates how the juxtaposition of light and dark tones, whether planned or accidental, can produce different geometric effects. Studying the quilt surface as a whole, the viewer may see hexagons, six-pointed stars, or pyramids, depending on the group of triangles observed. These illusionary effects are likely to have been accidental, since this seems to be a scrap bag quilt, albeit pieced of costly silk fabrics, prepared without an overall plan of tonal coordination that would have resulted in a more uniform design scheme. (*Author's collection.*)

Fig. 3.33. Footprints in the Sands of Time (Jacob's Ladder variation) pattern pieced quilt, Amish, c. 1890. Mifflin County, Pennsylvania. Made by Mrs. Samuel Sharp. 81″ x 68″. Cotton sateen. As its evocative name suggests, this quilt features lines coursing in every direction and different elements vying to dominate the visual field. Using the simplest shapes and tonal combinations, the quilter has produced an intricate network from blocks. Black provides a rich contrast to the lighter shades which form the four- and nine-patch blocks and the triangular fillers. A diagonal grid seems both to dominate the surface and to be subordinate to a square grid that weaves over and under the myriad pieces. (*Photo courtesy Barbara S. Janos and Barbara Ross.*)

3.31

3.32

3.33

Diamonds and Cubes

BOTH THE DIAMOND and the cube are variations of the square patch, but with angled sides that naturally add a dynamic quality to any design, since an angle automatically implies motion or depth.

A diamond is a four-sided figure, which can be equilateral—that is, with sides of equal length—or composed of elongated sides. Some diamonds are formed simply by turning squares on point.

In quiltmaking, the cube is a multiple patch formed of three diamonds, one of which is usually employed horizontally, and two of which are set at an angle. This grouping can be treated as one unit by using the same color for all three pieces, or by varying the shading, using two or three different colored or patterned fabrics within the unit to achieve a wide variety of optical effects. If the colors of the diamonds incorporated in a cube are varied, a sense of volume or depth results. If only one fabric is used for the piecing, the form will read like a hexagon.

The Tumbling Blocks cube design is the most familiar to quilt lovers. It is also called Stair Steps or Illusion and, most commonly in the South, Baby Blocks, and is the pattern most frequently acknowledged as capable of revealing an optical illusion, even in quilt studies compiled nearly a century ago.

If volume can be suggested in just one cube unit, imagine the sense of depth that can be communicated when cubes are repeated by the hundreds, and even thousands, as is quite common in quiltmaking. The architectural impression achieved in such repetition can be astonishing. By skillfully handling the colors of each cube, the quiltmaker can create tremendously powerful graphic designs, in many of which the top of one cube serves also as the bottom of the cube in the row above it. The entertaining visual confusion and constant shifts in perception that result are a hallmark of quilts of illusion.

Both the diamond and the cube are more difficult to piece than the straight-sided square because their angled sides require the quilter to cut the fabric on the bias. In so doing she could easily stretch the fabric, thus distorting the subsequent composition. Each angled side of a diamond or cube must be precisely measured to insure that contiguous pieces align properly and that the finished quilt top will lie flat.

FIG. 3.34. Leavenworth Star pattern pieced quilt, detail, c. 1920, Pennsylvania. Maker unknown. 88″ x 86″. Cotton. This captivating, intricate composition, full of pattern and depth, is simply constructed, repeating one pieced block several hundred times. That block has an eight-pointed star at its center, and a mitered border in which each side is pieced of three patches (two diamonds and a rhomboid). At each intersection of four such blocks, the diamonds link up to form another star pattern, which advances in the viewer's perception as four three-dimensional cubes. One's eye constantly shifts from the stars in the blocks to the stars at the intersections to the diagonal starry grid above a squared-off field. The sensation of depth is accentuated because all the elements look as if they have beveled edges. Patterned turn-of-the-century cottons comprise the more than 1,500 pieces in the quilt. It would be interesting to see the same design executed in solid fabrics. (*Author's collection.*)

FIG. 3.35. Trip Around the World (Sunshine and Shadow variation) pattern pieced quilt, Amish, c. 1900, Lancaster County, Pennsylvania. Maker unknown. 78″ x 76″. Cotton. A classic Pennsylvania-Amish design has been transformed through the use of shading to read like interwoven strips reaching back into a vortex, rather than as the concentrically pulsating diamonds with which this pattern is identified. Small diamonds in dusty tones merge in many areas and appear to undulate over and under each other. This unique visual effect probably occurred by accident as the quilter used up the scraps at hand; it is doubtful that the fabrics were carefully coordinated. (*Private collection; photo courtesy Judith & James Milne.*)

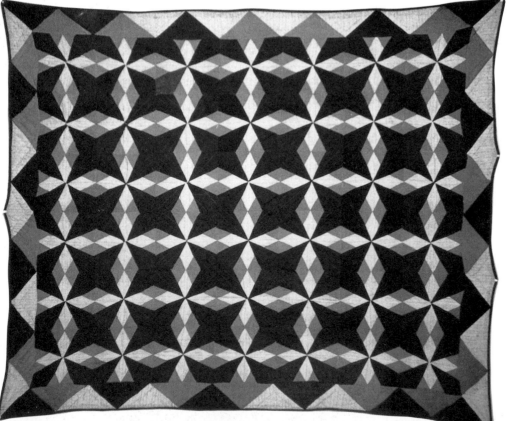

FIG. 3.36. Travel Star pattern pieced quilt, c. 1910. Texas. Maker unknown. 76″ x 64″. Wool. Each block of this dynamic quilt is centered with a four-pointed star made of dark wool suiting and is surrounded by lighter shades of diamonds. The strong, shifting images which activate the quilt surface emerge only when the blocks are joined. Together, these elements produce a pattern similar in effect to figures 1.6 and 4.1, in which several geometric designs vie for attention. The stars look as if set in octagonal rings, while elongated medium- and light-toned four-pointed stars emerge from a dark ground. Most wool quilts of this era were made for warmth from available clothing scraps, but this quilt's maker must have sensed the dramatic possibilities that lay in the contrasting wools she probably chose especially for this design. (*Author's collection.*)

FIGS. 3.37, 3.38. Touching Stars pattern pieced quilt and detail, c. 1883, Shelbyville, Tennessee. Made by Charlotte Waite Burditt. 95¼″ x 78¼″. Cotton. What looks at first glance like a series of Indian tepees or hexagons centered with stars is actually an imaginative large-scale composition of six-pointed stars. The variety of visual images stems from color juxtaposition and pattern repetition. The pale shades of the many diamonds in the arms of the stars cause them to merge with the background and exaggerates the darker aspects of the piecing. In addition, those areas converge perceptually like a diagonal grid framing hexagonal images. The stars disintegrate into other elements of the total composition until close inspection, when each intricately pieced six-pointed shape emerges. (*Collection of Charlotte N. Parrish; photo courtesy Quilts of Tennessee.*)

FIG. 3.39. Broken Star pattern pieced quilt, Amish, c. 1935, Holmes County, Ohio. Maker unknown. 89" x 79". Cotton. Three Amish quilts of the Broken Star pattern have been chosen to demonstrate the different visual possibilities inherent in the same design. In this first example, the choice of colors and their juxtaposition causes the design to appear less dense, even though all three versions probably contain the same number of diamond patches. The eye tends to focus here on the outside "star" ring, where bright patches link with the star arms to read like tufts or pompoms independent of the overall design. The lavender diamonds of the field between the star arms recede visually, as if these areas have been cut out of the quilt, rather than advancing as they do when black is used. (*Photo courtesy Darwin D. Bearley.*)

FIG. 3.40. Broken Star pattern pieced quilt, Amish, c. 1930, Holmes County, Ohio. Maker unknown. 79″ square. Cotton sateen. This example of the Broken Star shows how the inner and outer points of the star form can be made to seemingly burst out toward the quilt's edges rather than to be contained within its borders. The outer ring, pieced of diamonds, appears to be a series of serrated star-tipped forms because the diamond patches relate in palette. The black fields between the inner and outer piecing seem to have acquired points themselves as they link up with the black diamonds in the surrounding pieced area. (*Photo courtesy Darwin D. Bearley.*)

FIG. 3.41. Broken Star pattern pieced quilt, Amish, c. 1935, Holmes County, Ohio. Maker unknown. 90″ square. Cotton. Chromatic juxtapositions can produce a variety of optical effects. In this bold version of the Broken Star pattern, the eight-pointed star at the center nearly disappears amid the turbulence of the design. Two distinct elements advance. The large black diamonds (which are actually the ground or field between the star arms and the pieced surround) seem to float above the quilt surface; the pieced border reads like a scalloped ring or a network of intertwined links encircling the star, rather than as an extension of the central pattern. (*Photo courtesy Darwin D. Bearley.*)

FIG. 3.42. Zigzag (One-Patch variation) pattern pieced quilt, c. 1885, Berks County, Pennsylvania. Maker unknown. 80″ x 71″. Cotton. This unusual variation of a simple one-patch pattern is dazzling, its visible yet invisible lines and angles calling to mind heat waves rising from a hot summer pavement. Another Pennsylvania quilter might have taken these pieced diamond elements and turned them into a conventional Star of Bethlehem, but this anonymous artist gathered the diamond groups into bars and joined them with vertical strips pieced of two more diamonds, creating a chevron-like, kinetic composition. (*Collection of M. Finkel & Daughter.*)

FIG. 3.43. Triple Irish Chain pattern pieced quilt, Amish, c. 1905, Holmes County, Ohio. Maker unknown. 79″ x 65″. Cotton. Through the phenomenon of closure, the eye perceives big black dots in this sophisticated but disarmingly simple design. They appear to be either afloat on, or dropped out of, a checkered field which is the classic pieced design. Although the black areas have angular sides, they read as circular because the eye tries to compensate for the distortion and to justify the contrast between the vast expanse of black and the lighter surround. (*Photo courtesy Darwin D. Bearley.*)

FIG. 3.44. Arkansas Traveler pattern pieced quilt, c. 1880, Ohio. Maker unknown. 82″ square. Wool challis. The quilter's choice of just three contrasting fabrics results in design variations more clearly defined and dramatic than they would be if many fabrics had been employed. The viewer perceives four-pointed stars set within dotted octagons, but these motifs soon lose the competition for visual dominance to lighter diagonal bands which traverse the quilt surface. A somewhat shallow sense of depth is conveyed where pinwheels cover pointed stars. All this geometric effect has been accomplished using only two diamond-shaped pattern pieces—one elongated, the other, kite-like. (*Private collection; photo courtesy of the author.*)

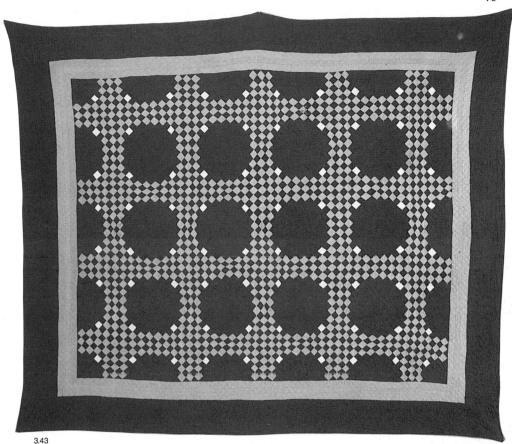

3.43

3.44

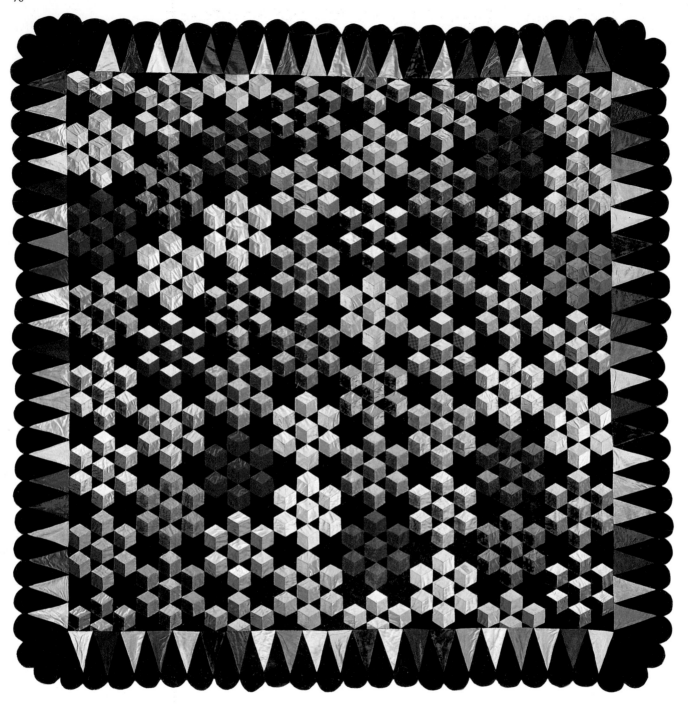

FIG. 3.45. Tumbling Blocks and Stars pattern pieced quilt, c. 1880, Portsmouth, Ohio. Made by Mrs. James Newman. 78″ x 74″. Silk and velvet. Seven cubes, arranged in a hexagonal grouping, touch to surround black velvet six-pointed stars. These geometric forms compete for visual dominance, and the quilt surface is in constant motion as these elements either advance or recede. In addition, the cubes' formations provoke differing spatial perceptions depending on the greater or lesser color contrasts within. Some appear as if seen from above; some, as if seen from the side; and others, as flattened hexagonal elements. This skillful and un-common treatment of Baby Blocks shows the extent to which a variety of effects can be achieved through the choice of colors and fabrics. (*Collection of Mr. & Mrs. M. Curtis; photo courtesy Stella Rubin.*)

FIG. 3.46. Tumbling Blocks pattern pieced quilt, Amish, c. 1930, Holmes County, Ohio. Maker unknown. Dimensions unavailable. Wool and cotton. The subdued palette of blues, violet, maroon, mustard, and green in this cubic composition emits a very different visual impression from the light-hearted, delicate example of figure 3.47. The pattern plays visual tricks at several levels of the quilt surface because of color similarity or contrast. Where closer in value, the rows read like horizontal strings of diamonds atop dark, undulating ribbons, as if viewed from above. Where more contrasting, the rows read as three-dimensional cubes seen from either the right, left, or above. The variation in shading transforms the basic cube from two dimensions to three as color contrast increases. Admirers of contemporary art may appreciate the architectural variations of shape and color, but the quilter probably had no such goal in mind—she used whatever shades were available. (*Photo courtesy Judi Boisson Antique American Quilts.*)

FIG. 3.47. Tumbling Blocks pattern pieced quilt, Amish, c. 1940, Michigan. Maker unknown. Dimensions unavailable. Cotton sateen. A pastel rainbow of cubes in striped rows reads simultaneously from above and below, from right and left, because of the color juxtapositions. Some of the bold, three-dimensional cubes have darkly shadowed left sides which suggest movement in that direction, while others march sprightly to the right; the direction constantly seems to switch. The overall illusion presented suggests a space-age weave of assorted high-tech colors, rather than the straightforward alignment of cubes that would have emerged if fewer colors had been employed. (*Photo courtesy Judi Boisson Antique American Quilts.*)

FIG. 3.48. Seven Sisters (Tumbling Blocks variation) pattern pieced quilt, c. 1875, Pennsylvania. Maker unknown. 82" x 80". Cotton. Six-pointed stars ringed by white hexagons are compressed into a multi-thousand piece composition that is actually a tiny Tumbling Blocks pattern. The blocks keep shifting into stars and back into blocks. The visual intrigue is compounded by the strong directional lines that have been generated by carefully coordinating the cubes' sides in the same fabrics so they link up across or diagonally upon the quilt surface. Even the stars vary as we study the design: some, in medium-tone Victorian calicoes, appear full bodied, while others seem to be composed of trilobed forms of white diamonds. (*Author's collection.*)

3.48

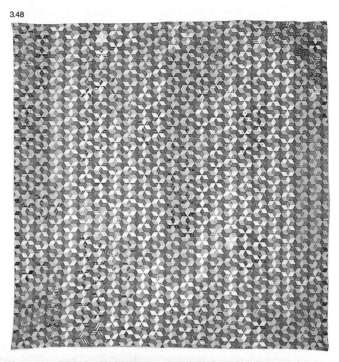

FIG. 3.49. Tumbling Blocks pattern pieced quilt, Mennonite, c. 1880, Pennsylvania. Maker unknown. 76" x 66". Wool. A variety of solid woolens has been incorporated in this un-patterned blocks variation. Both cubes and six-pointed stars become visible, but with no particular consistency. The diamond-shaped pieces are probably clothing remnants, making this quilt a true scrap composition. The cubes here were probably treated independently, rather than orchestrated by tone to further a grander design scheme. (*Photo courtesy Esprit Quilt Collection.*)

3.49

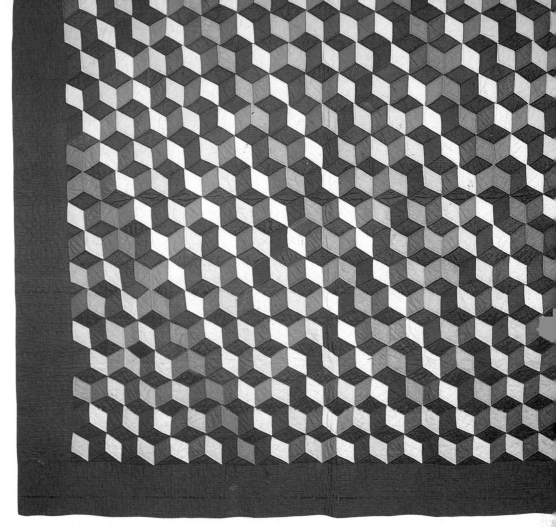

FIG. 3.50. Illusion (Tumbling Blocks variation) pattern pieced quilt. Amish, c. 1930, Holmes County, Ohio. Maker unknown. Dimensions unavailable. Cotton. Forceful diagonals, like streamers, are as dominant visually as the traditional cubes of this design. They read as ribbons, blocks, or rows, depending upon the variation in placement of the light, medium, and dark diamonds. The optical effect shifts particularly at the upper right and lower left corners in this dynamic and continually changing creation. (*Private collection; photo courtesy Esprit Quilt Collection.*)

FIG. 3.51. Tumbling Blocks pattern pieced quilt, Amish, c. 1935, Holmes County, Ohio. Maker unknown. 80″ x 76″. Cotton. Because almost all of the cubes in this traditional pattern are topped with identical fabric diamonds, the quilt surface appears as if it were a three-dimensional composition observed from above. The absence of coordination of the medium and dark tones at the sides of the cubes restricts our perception to this more singular spatial illusion. The blocks seem to have been constructed as scraps became available, without adherence to a more formal scheme that might have organized the various intensities of shading. (*Photo courtesy Esprit Quilt Collection.*)

FIG. 3.52. Stairway to Heaven (Tumbling Blocks variation) pattern pieced quilt, Amish, c. 1940, Midwest. Maker unknown. Dimensions unavailable. Cotton. This masterpiece of color coordination and composition is aptly named. The eye is carried up and in and out of the quilt surface by the blocks which form the "stairs," as each diagonal row leads to a distant point seemingly beyond the quilt's borders. The design reads as steps whether right side up or upside down. Right side up, the stairs point in from both sides to create an inverted "V" peak; upside down, two sets of stairs diverge from a lower point beyond the quilt edges. In some blocks or cubes, the top diamonds are the lightest; in others, the two lower are identically colored; in still others, all three are the same color, but of different intensities. Yet all read as three-dimensional objects, conveying a feeling of depth and space. (*Photo courtesy Esprit Quilt Collection.*)

FIG. 3.53. Hexagonal Star pattern pieced quilt, c. 1880, Cumberland County, Kentucky. Made by Mary Alexander. 91" x 76½". Cotton. A close look at the little stars that seem to be set within hexagons reveals that each is composed of three cubes whose bases touch. Because of the varying color relationships of the Victorian prints used, some of these read clearly as stars, while others read as cubes in three dimension. By filling the spaces between the hexagonal segments with triangles of a lighter hue, the quiltmaker has created yet another geometric image—that of a larger six-pointed star in which each hexagon is centered. (*Photo courtesy of The Kentucky Quilt Project, Inc.*)

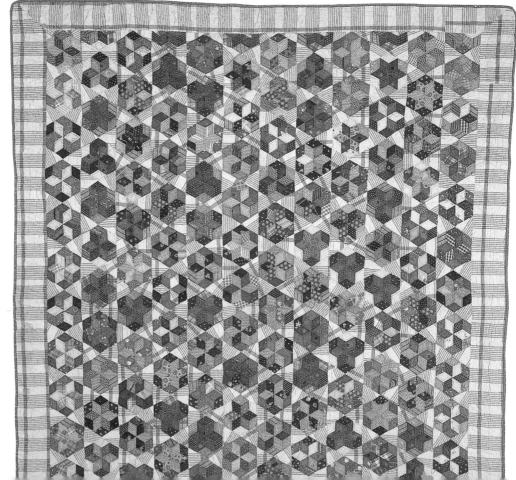

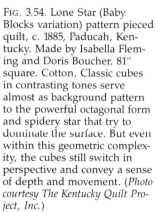

FIG. 3.54. Lone Star (Baby Blocks variation) pattern pieced quilt, c. 1885, Paducah, Kentucky. Made by Isabella Fleming and Doris Boucher. 81″ square. Cotton. Classic cubes in contrasting tones serve almost as background pattern to the powerful octagonal form and spidery star that try to dominate the surface. But even within this geometric complexity, the cubes still switch in perspective and convey a sense of depth and movement. (*Photo courtesy The Kentucky Quilt Project, Inc.*)

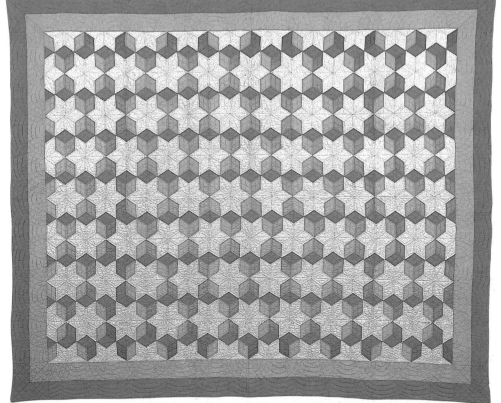

FIG. 3.55. Tumbling Blocks (Columbia Star variation) pattern pieced quilt, c. 1930, Ohio. Maker unknown. 90″ x 80″. Cotton. A restricted palette of complementary shades allows for sharp visualization of distinct tumbling blocks which seem to move around a series of white six-pointed stars. A similar construction is shown in figures 3.45 and 3.98. If the quilt is read vertically as originally designed, the blocks appear as a hexagonal surround for the stars; when read horizontally, the cubes appear to have been organized in zigzag rows with the deepest shade as their axis. (*Author's collection.*)

Rectangles and Strips

A RECTANGLE is a straight-sided figure in which the length exceeds the width, or vice versa. It is also defined as a four-sided figure with four right angles. In quiltmaking, strips are longer, narrower pieces of rectangular shape, such as those most familiarly seen in Log Cabin patterns. The rectangular shape can either be cut directly from cloth, or communicated visually by joining two or more squares of identical fabric to create the elongated element.

The boldest geometric quilt employing rectangles or strips is known as a Bars pattern. It is frequently made by needleworkers of the Amish and Mennonite sects, who arrange full length strips of fabric across the quilt surface. More common are abbreviated pieced bars, which enable a thrifty seamstress to incorporate small scraps of many printed or solid-color fabrics into a simple design. Using even a minimal two-color scheme, a quilter can combine rectangular patches and rotate them in direction according to a consistent plan to develop powerful graphic designs.

Log Cabin pattern variations are among the most versatile of quilt designs using rectangles or strips. They permit the quiltmaker to combine hundreds and sometimes thousands of strips to achieve limitless results just by coordinating the light and dark tonalities of the materials within the composition. The strips can be composed of scrap fabric in a multitude of prints or can be limited to a two- or three-color palette chosen to effect a particular visual goal. Such quilts' construction echoes the log shelter which became commonplace as colonists moved westward across the North American continent. Made in a fashion that emulates that building, the basic log cabin blocks contain strips surrounding a central square that symbolizes the hearth around which the home was built.

The Log Cabin pattern is a practical one, because it enables the completion of a quilt from small, otherwise useless scraps. It is also portable, since it can be composed of manageable blocks with no necessity to create complicated templates. Log Cabin quilts, though commonplace projects among mid- to late-nineteenth-century seamstresses, are remarkable for their variety, a variety made possible by the originality with which each quiltmaker orchestrated the placement of light- and dark-toned fabrics.

FIG. 3.56. Log Cabin (Courthouse Steps variation) pattern pieced quilt, c. 1850, New England. Maker unknown. Dimensions unavailable. Wool. Thousands of multi-patterned log strips compose small diamonds that have been combined without attention to a large-scale contrasting color scheme as is usual in more traditional Courthouse Steps variations. The result is an intricate, richly colored, almost textural composition that looks like ribbons of fabric woven over and under to create a whole cloth. In various areas of the quilt, crisscross images surface because of the harmony or contrast of neighboring strips. (*Photo courtesy Judi Boisson Antique American Quilts.*)

FIG. 3.57. Roman Wall pattern pieced quilt, c. 1895, locale unknown. Maker unknown. 45″ x 32″. Silk and velvet. This dramatic crib quilt looks as if an iron grid had compressed an array of fabrics so that they splashed out in all directions from its weight. In actuality, this sophisticated stained-glass-like creation, which the owner calls his "Franz Kline painting," has been made in blocks of wedge-like strips of fabric pieced as if they radiated from one corner. Their direction has been rotated almost symmetrically when joined, so that the narrow strips convey a subordinate illusion of concentric diamonds or four-pointed stars beneath the black grid which borders them. (*Photo courtesy Darwin D. Bearley.*)

FIG. 3.58. Carpenter's Square pattern pieced quilt, c. 1890, locale unknown. Maker unknown. 79″ square. Cotton. Resembling a classic meander or Greek key pattern in which a consistent geometric form interlocks, this maze-like design was created by the careful organization of narrow strips of just two fabrics. A sequence of layers is suggested in which a central square of interlacing appears to have been applied to a dark sawtooth area which tops a white ground, or vice versa. The lines and points communicate so much movement and interruption of image that the viewer cannot extract the figure from its field. Traditionally, this pattern employs dark strips on white; here the treatment has been reversed and the design so compacted that we are continually mystified as to what lies over or under, what is connected or separate, and what is moving in or out. (*Photo courtesy Darwin D. Bearley.*)

3.59

3.60

Fig. 3.59. Snail's Trails pattern pieced quilt, c. 1875, Pennsylvania. Maker unknown. 80″ x 79″. Cotton. Thousands of nineteenth-century, richly colored calico prints have been pieced in strips and organized to interlock visually, making it impossible for the viewer to judge which element predominates: the lines arching over and around, or under and up. The quiltmaker achieved a symmetry of composition that is remarkable in light of the blindingly small scale and dense patterning of the strips. In one of those rare designs whose pattern name truly reflects the image from which it has been drawn, the quilt surface is in constant motion, its squiggly lines leading the eye around an enigmatic, endless maze. (*Photo courtesy Darwin D. Bearley.*)

Fig. 3.60. Stars in a Diamond out of a Square pattern pieced quilt, c. 1920, probably Southern. Maker unknown. 72″ square. Silk and rayon. The whimsical title given by the current owner to her exuberant discovery conveys the quilt's three-dimensional trick imagery. The design has been pieced primarily of strips for the framework and large star, diamonds in the center star, and triangles to fill in. Nothing has been layered, yet the viewer perceives the major design elements as separate entities. It seems as if the quiltmaker created tiny glazier's points to hold down the black octagon that outlines the center stars, but nothing can visually contain the explosive eccentricity of the composition. (*Collection of Susan Parrish Antiques.*)

3.61

3.62

FIG. 3.61. Hayes' Corner pattern pieced quilt, Amish, c. 1930. Ohio. Maker unknown. 80″ x 72″. Cotton. The entire background, composed of narrow pastel strips, seems to be rotating like the sleeve-clad arms of a windmill, despite the imaginary efforts of the black "bars" to pin the composition in place. The sense of movement results from the strips having been organized into quadrants whose direction alternates from vertical to horizontal. The "barn raising" (black diamond) element seen here, for which this pattern is frequently mistaken, emerges from black strips which have been carefully aligned to follow the direction of their background section. It is interesting to compare this variation with figures 3.26 and 3.121, where the pattern is developed more traditionally using triangles, squares, and strips to generate the concentric diamonds. (*Photo courtesy Darwin D. Bearley.*)

FIG. 3.62. Joseph's Coat pattern pieced quilt, dated 1893, Pennsylvania. Initialed E.G.G. 88″ x 80″. Cotton. This spare, classic quilt appears to be bent at the ends, as if it has been photographed draped on top of a box. It looks like an isometric projection, rather than the flat surface of a simple quilt. This optical whimsy has been created through the quilter's innovative decision to align the colors in the top and bottom borders so as to extend the colors of the bars within the quilt body. Traditionally, the border is set out diagonally around the body without coordinating the colors, to show a clear separation between those areas. (*Collection of Susan Parrish Antiques.*)

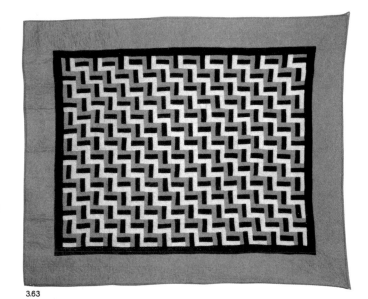

3.63

FIG. 3.63. Fence Rail pattern (Endless Stair variation) pieced quilt, Amish, dated 1927, LaGrange County, Indiana. Maker unknown. Dimensions unavailable. Cotton. Stair steps in light and medium shades alternately pop and sizzle down the quilt surface, casting dark shadows that underscore the illusion of depth this pattern suggests. It appears as if an unseen light source has activated this composition, which is based on the simple construct of making square blocks of three strips in contrasting tones, then rotating the direction of every other one. The Fence Rail pattern usually reads like interwoven striped ribbons, but here the limited palette and the use of black generate a constantly switching three-dimensional illusion. (*Collection of David and Eva Wheatcroft.*)

FIG. 3.64. Unnamed design pieced quilt, c. 1875, Pennsylvania. Maker unknown. 85" x 75". Cotton. Looking more like an engraving or etching than a construction in fabric, this maze of pattern may be the quiltmaker's personal artistic vision of an eight-pointed star or of spoked wheels. The octagonal shapes do not remain distinct in the viewer's perception for very long, because the diagonal "spokes" direct the eye through an intricate network of pattern comprised of thousands of narrow strips of Victorian printed fabric. Between the octagons, forms like Celtic crosses also advance and recede. This visual illusion has been achieved solely with line, rather than light and dark tonal contrasts. It is most unusual, sharing its dramatic, graphic originality with Snail's Trails (fig. 3.59), another turbulent masterpiece. (*Photo courtesy Darwin D. Bearley.*)

3.64

Log Cabin Variations

SIX PRINCIPAL VARIATIONS of the Log Cabin pattern are commonly found in quiltmaking, but even two identically named quilts, using the same methods of construction, can appear quite different because of the color and fabric groupings chosen by the quilter who created them. Several examples of some variations are included here to demonstrate the optical variety that is the hallmark of this format.

In the Barn Raising variation, the surface reads as diamonds of light and dark tones radiating concentrically from a central, solid diamond core. The log cabin blocks have been bisected diagonally into triangular light or dark areas and then combined. The successively larger tonal outlines that result convey the illusion of movement.

A different juxtaposition of blocks produces alternating diamonds which appear as solid light and dark shapes. Typically, the Light and Dark variation is composed by first grouping four blocks, in each of which the tones are arranged in triangular areas. When joined so that the lights or darks meet to create corresponding diamonds, and then united with further groups of four blocks, diamonds of the opposing tone emerge at the intersections.

A rotation of the Light and Dark scheme produces the Straight Furrow variation, in which the contrasting triangular halves abut and vary to generate diagonal swathes across the quilt surface. With another twist, the Straight Furrow becomes the Streak of Lightning or Zigzag variation, in which the bands of contrasting shades turn back and forth.

When the log cabin block is divided by lights and darks horizontally and vertically, rather than diagonally, a different variation called Courthouse Steps emerges. The illusion is of strips of decreasing length leading up to a center square.

In the Windmill Blades or Pineapple variation, the strips within the log cabin block can be arranged either in a cross or X fashion. The ends of the strips are clipped at an angle to suggest motion. Because its execution entails difficult and precise piecing and assembly, this variation is perhaps the most dynamic and unusual of the Log Cabin patterns.

Many of these intriguing variations are difficult to decipher, because the structural log cabin blocks are sublimated to the bold visual imagery of the light and dark shapes that form the illusions. By focusing on the central hearth square and following the strips outward from it, the viewer can understand how the groups of log cabin blocks were juxtaposed and maneuvered to create an unusual quilt design. Sometimes two or more block variations were employed in one quilt to produce a dramatic, unusual composition.

FIG. 3.65. Log Cabin (Light and Dark variation) pattern pieced quilt detail, c. 1880, locale unknown. Maker unknown. Dimensions unavailable. Silk satin. The construction of log cabin blocks proceeds differently from other designs. A method known as "press piecing" is used, in which the strips are sewn to and through a foundation cloth block. The pattern is built up around a central square, which represents the hearth. The first log strip is sewn face down to the square, then folded and pressed back. The quilt block, typically from 10″ to 14″ square, progresses as each piece is attached in the same fashion, perpendicular to the previous strip. One block can contain as few as nine strips or as many as fifty. The placement of light and dark strips within each block and the juxtaposition of the blocks as they are joined makes possible almost unlimited variations of the Log Cabin pattern. (*Photo courtesy The Main Street Press.*)

FIG. 3.66. Log Cabin (Barn Raising variation) pattern pieced quilt, c. 1875, Pennsylvania. Maker unknown. 88″ x 82″. Cotton. In this pristine classic example, approximately 5,000 quarter-inch strips of patterned Victorian cottons have been coordinated in concentric diamonds of light and dark which vie for attention as they expand to the edges of the quilt surface. The tiny prints are so harmonious in scale that nothing breaks the pattern's symmetry, yet each is clearly legible within the larger contrasting graphic design. (*Collection of Steven Gross; photo courtesy of the author.*)

FIG. 3.67. Log Cabin (mini-Barn Raising variation) pattern pieced quilt, c. 1875, locale unknown. Maker unknown. 90″ x 75″. Wool challis. The familiar large-scale Barn Raising variation has here been pieced in miniature and repeated thirty times across the quilt surface to create a geometric puzzle whose design seems to overlap its boundaries. This effect has been achieved through the placement of the diagonals in relation to the outermost strips which frame each square and through tonal contrasts which heighten the illusion that small diamonds have been set atop square backgrounds. When the strips are close in value, they seem to radiate at their centers. Others, pieced of contrasting fabrics, are boldly outlined. (*Photo courtesy Darwin D. Bearley.*)

FIG. 3.68. Log Cabin (Straight Furrow variation) pattern pieced quilt, c. 1925, locale unknown. Maker unknown. 80″ x 75″. Cotton. Designs are perceived on several planes simultaneously in this unique variation. A checkerboard-like pattern of gray squares alternating with split green and yellow squares seems to surmount the classic imagery of the Straight Furrow pattern as it courses diagonally beneath in bands that are predominantly yellow or gray. Try as we might to fix our focus on one or the other pattern, those designs surface equally in a compelling illusion whose vintage colors and pattern emerge as a strikingly contemporary geometric wonder. This one-of-a-kind quilt seems deceptively simple to make: a square block has been divided in half diagonally by light and dark, alternated with a solid block, and united by a white sashing that appears as a light overlying grid. (*Photo courtesy Darwin D. Bearley.*)

3.68

3.69

FIG. 3.69. Log Cabin (unpatterned variation) pattern pieced quilt, c. 1940, Ohio. Maker unknown. 86″ x 72″. Rayon. Pieced of strips from men's ties in wonderful Art Deco and Moderne designs, this funky variation has been compiled with no regard for the light and dark tonalities that when organized generate an overall graphic pattern. It is included to demonstrate how Log Cabin variations depend for their illusionary impact upon the contrast of tone and value. Even without a scheme, however, this unusual quilt can still be enjoyed for its aesthetic similarity to such movements of modern art as Italian Impressionism or Abstract Expressionism, and for its own excitement. (*Author's collection.*)

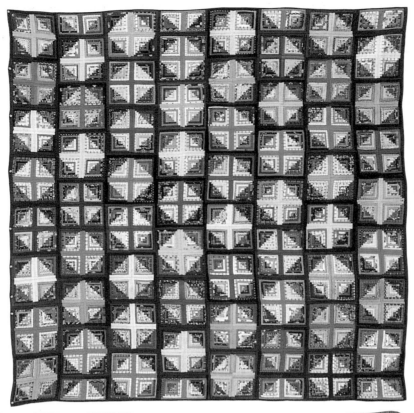

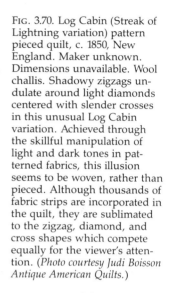

FIG. 3.70. Log Cabin (Streak of Lightning variation) pattern pieced quilt, c. 1850, New England. Maker unknown. Dimensions unavailable. Wool challis. Shadowy zigzags undulate around light diamonds centered with slender crosses in this unusual Log Cabin variation. Achieved through the skillful manipulation of light and dark tones in patterned fabrics, this illusion seems to be woven, rather than pieced. Although thousands of fabric strips are incorporated in the quilt, they are sublimated to the zigzag, diamond, and cross shapes which compete equally for the viewer's attention. (*Photo courtesy Judi Boisson Antique American Quilts.*)

FIG. 3.71. Log Cabin (Streak of Lightning variation) pattern pieced quilt, c. 1920, locale unknown. Maker unknown. 82″ x 80″. Cotton. Resembling an antique Navaho blanket or Indian serape or other woven textile, this pieced Log Cabin quilt has a graphic vigor and sophisticated design emphasized by its restricted palette (blue and white). The central design seems to reverberate, with the light and dark outlines conveying a reversible illusion. Although the quilt surface appears to be constantly in motion, the viewer can locate the square blocks from which the design was built by seeking out the tiny dark squares at their centers. (*Photo courtesy Esprit Quilt Collection.*)

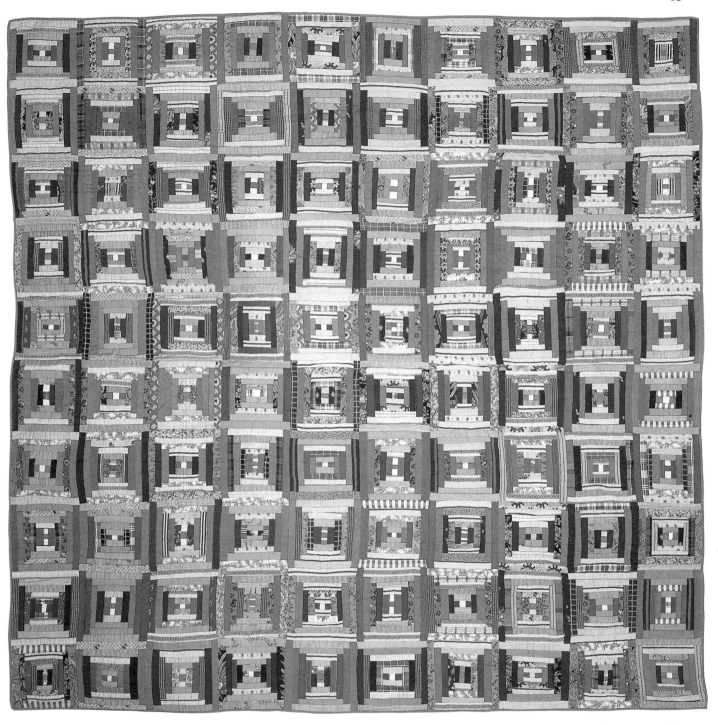

FIG. 3.72. Log Cabin (Court-house Steps variation) pattern pieced quilt, c. 1875, locale unknown. Maker unknown. Dimensions unavailable. Wool. Tesselated diamonds in light and dark tones vie for atten-tion as they pop out of and back into a richly patterned and intricately pieced surface. In this classic variation, thousands of scraps from Vic-torian gowns were joined in square blocks with the lights and darks set out on opposite sides, rather than to one side as in a Barn Raising (fig. 3.66) or Light and Dark (fig. 1.14) variation. The "serrated" edges of the diamonds sometimes merge in our perception as diagonal woven lines, adding to the optical illusions this unusual quilt produces. (*Collec-tion of Tewksbury Antiques.*)

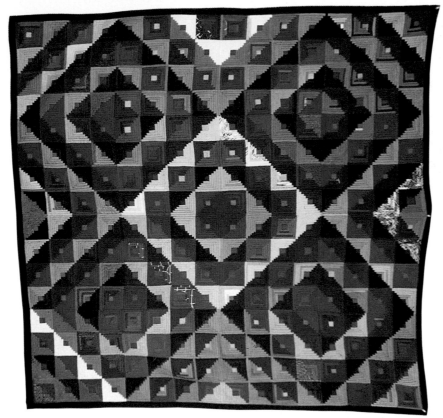

Fig. 3.73. Log Cabin (Barn Raising variation) pattern pieced quilt, c. 1900, locale unknown. Maker unknown. 74″ square. Wool. Shadowy, pulsating layers of pattern convey a great kinetic sense in this unusual variation. Rather than presenting sharply defined lights and darks, the elements here are treated like triangles (as in the Delectable Mountains pattern, figure 3.30) to produce large overlapping diamonds which veil underlying colors. In this mysterious, almost architectural, composition, the central area with its red diamond seems to move out and back as it competes with the four surrounding areas for visual dominance. The pointed edges of all design elements serve to keep the surface in motion. (*Photo courtesy Darwin D. Bearley.*)

Fig. 3.74. Log Cabin (Pineapple variation) pattern pieced quilt, Amish, c. 1925, Ohio. Maker unknown. 82″ x 75″. Cotton. In the typical Pineapple configuration, the perceived pattern switches from light to dark four-pointed forms, but this unusual version presents additional graphic images. Pale diamonds with dark outlines, stars, and circles are visible in addition to the four-pointed Pineapple forms. All the curves, points, and extensions of the pattern keep the surface in motion. (*Photo courtesy Judi Boisson Antique American Quilts.*)

3.75

3.76

FIG. 3.75. Log Cabin (Barn Raising variation) pattern pieced quilt, c. 1875, locale unknown. 86″ x 78″. Wool. Outlined diamonds in light, medium, and dark shades appear successively to frame a central pale diamond and then to terminate beyond the borders of this classic variation. At the same time, the little dark squares at the center of each structural block seem to float independent of the quilt surface, as if photographed in 3-D. (*Photo courtesy Darwin D. Bearley.*)

FIG. 3.76. Log Cabin (Courthouse Steps variation) pattern pieced quilt, c. 1875, locale unknown. Maker unknown. 78″ x 72″. Cotton. In this unusual variation, the large-scale image has been transformed into an elongated, interlocking chain rather than a squared-off design. The lights and darks on opposite sides of the blocks are so uniform in color that they exaggerate the sense of dark links advancing toward the viewer, but from another perspective they recede while white Chinese lantern-like forms seem to take center stage. (*Photo courtesy Darwin D. Bearley.*)

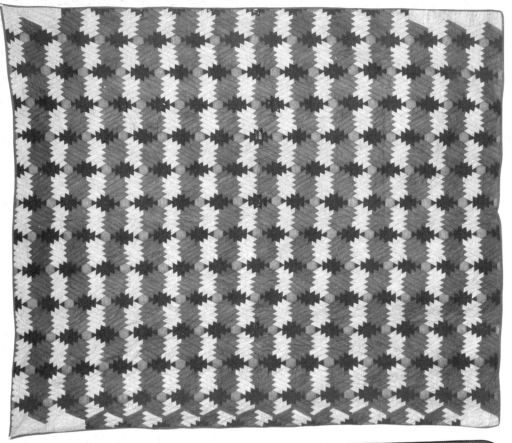

Fig. 3.77. Log Cabin (Church Steps variation) pattern pieced quilt, c. 1860, Tennessee. Maker unknown. 86″ x 74″. Wool challis. Log Cabin quilts are typically two-toned— composed of light and dark fabrics. In this variation, the quilter has introduced a rare third tone to her choice and arrangement of fabric strips to create a complex composition. Horizontals and verticals read simultaneously. Stripes of pale- and medium-toned fabrics alternate in one direction and seem to be woven in the other direction through a "clasp" of black. These visuals emerge because the composition is based on a structure of three: each pattern block is a hexagon rather than a square, divided into three colors (either rust-black-rust or camel-black-camel). In this unusual quilt, the center of each segment is truly three-dimensional: a pale (blue) scrap has been stuffed, giving the quilt tactile as well as visual surface intrigue. (*Author's collection.*)

Fig. 3.78. Log Cabin (Windmill Blades variation) pattern pieced quilt, c. 1875, locale unknown. Maker unknown. 89″ x 79″. Wool. Black "pro-pellers" emerging from bull's-eye targets on a dark field elevate this variation into an extraordinary graphic original. All aspects of the traditional pattern have been touched by this quiltmaker's creativity. The blocks have been set on point; the strips alternated by light and dark as well as opposed at the block corners rather than the sides; and the intersections filled in with diamonds. As a result, the quilt's images operate on several planes in intriguing complexity and endless appeal. (*Photo courtesy Darwin D. Bearley.*)

Fig. 3.79. Log Cabin (Barn Raising variation) pattern pieced quilt, c. 1890, locale unknown. Maker unknown. Dimensions unavailable. Cotton. The ripple effect of a pebble tossed into a pond may have been all the in-spiration needed for this reverberating design. While great waves of light and dark echo from the center diamonds (as in figures 3.66 and 3.75), rotating the outer log-cabin blocks breaks the light and

3.79

dark continuity and produces an innovative graphic. In addition, the careful alignment of light and dark strips within each log-cabin block expresses a subordinate zigzag pattern beneath the lighter, ripple-like elements. (*Photo courtesy Darwin D. Bearley.*)

FIG. 3.80. Log Cabin (Straight Furrow variation) pattern pieced quilt, c. 1880, Pennsylvania. Maker unknown. Dimensions unavailable. Wool. Shadowy diagonals appear either to veil, or to emerge

from, a design of repeating outlined squares in this unusual illusion. The diagonals have been created by alternating light and dark strips at one half of the structural blocks (on the diagonal) and alternating medium and dark strips at the other half, then aligning those complementary tones on the diagonal. The dramatic outlines of the pieced blocks suggest mazes spiraling in toward the black center squares from which each small block has been built. (*Photo courtesy Frank Ames.*)

3.80

Curvilinear and Hexagonal Forms

THE QUILT EXAMPLES grouped in this category feature patterns where the predominant line is curved, arched, or circular, even when composed of narrow strips or small patches. Hexagons, the six-sided figures, essentially read as rounded forms in illusionary quilts.

The curvilinear form that is probably the most familiar to quilt aficionados the world over is the Double Wedding Ring pattern. Curved edges are featured in all the narrow strips used to piece the rings and in the ground or field (typically of solid color) which centers the rings and forms the ellipses between their arcs, making such quilts more difficult to sew than those whose pieces have straight sides.

The Amish and other Wedding Ring examples featured here were chosen as quilts of illusion because they present either a sense of depth or of motion, due to their incorporation of highly contrasting colors or of solid fabrics darker than those typically seen in this pattern. (The classic implementation of this design uses sprightly pastel-patterned pieces with a light ground.) Our examples show that an innovative quilter with the courage to deviate from the norm can add spatial and kinetic dimensions to the most common pattern.

The hexagonal patch was most typically employed in the nineteenth century in an allover mosaic design sometimes referred to as English patchwork, which joins equal-size patches together without benefit of an organizing grid or other device, as is usually seen in American block work or square-patch designs. In the twentieth century, hexagons were most commonly grouped in a block of seven, where six hexagons of one color or fabric surround a seventh of different, usually solid, color which is kept consistent throughout the composition of the quilt surface. We know these as variations of the Grandmother's Flower Garden or French Bouquet patterns.

Because of the construction process necessary to create hexagonal designs, which employ hundreds or thousands of patches of identical size, there is little possibility for pattern variation. Consequently, there are far fewer examples of optical illusion quilts based on the true hexagon than of any other geometric form. The same observation holds true for most curvilinear designs. It is the straight-sided pieces, offering limitless possibilities for combination with other patches varied in size and shape, that have the greatest potential to become quilts of illusion.

FIG. 3.81. Rainbow (New York Beauty variation) pattern pieced quilt, c. 1890, Hickman County, Kentucky. Made by Ann Johnson Armstrong. 73″ x 68″. Cotton. Because this quilt masterpiece suggests curving gears and clockwork motion, it is included as an example of curvilinear forms despite its saw-toothed spikes and triangular elements. Each block has been constructed with a fan shape of many points filling nearly half the structural square from one corner. A magical optical effect has been created by varying the background colors and strategically coordinating the rotation of the blocks. The organization appears to be groups of double four patches, arranged by color and direction, which taken together read like cross sections of machinery gears. Through the perceptual phenomena of interrupted systems and closure, the viewer wants to mentally connect the rings. The owners call this quilt "Pull and Change of the Moon." (*Photo courtesy The Kentucky Quilt Project.*)

3.82

Fig. 3.82. World Without End (Drunkard's Path variation) pattern pieced quilt, c. 1885, locale unknown. Maker unknown. 80″ x 75″. Cotton. A variety of sophisticated graphic designs emerges in this carefully orchestrated composition. The viewer perceives a meandering diagonal interwoven grid, a four-leaf effect at some intersections, either a dark or light concave diamond-in-a-square at other areas, and a line of sinuous dark X's dancing repeatedly across the quilt surface. The quilt is a captivating puzzle that is a challenge to decipher. (*Photo courtesy Darwin D. Bearley.*)

3.83

Fig. 3.83. Drunkard's Path pattern pieced quilt, Amish, c. 1915, Wisconsin. Maker unknown. Dimensions unavailable. Cotton. This quilt's maker chose just two fabrics—one light (green), the other dark (red)—to create a constantly shifting optical puzzle. The dramatic figure/ground illusion confuses the viewer as to whether the dominant image is a dark diagonal grid or paler four-pointed forms. (*Photo courtesy Judi Boisson Antique American Quilts.*)

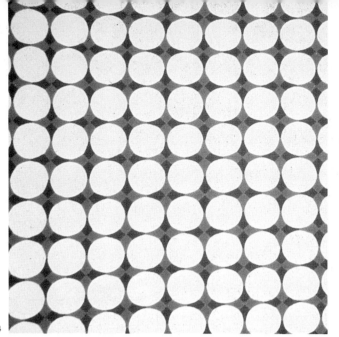

Fig. 3.84. Snowball (Four-Point variation) pattern pieced quilt, c. 1940, Sevier County, Tennessee. Made by Alice Parton. 74¼" x 57". Cotton. Tiny concave diamonds of four patches of dark cottons are united as stars whose points touch, forcing the eye to read great white dots as they intersect. The quilt's appearance varies, at once looking as if the maker had taken a hole punch to patterned fabric or laid white dots on top of a patterned ground. Many other names are given to this pattern, including Hummingbird, Kite, and Job's Troubles. (*Collection of Dell Reagan Compton; photo courtesy Quilts of Tennessee.*)

3.84

Fig. 3.85. Dolley Madison's Reel pattern pieced quilt, c. 1860, New York. Maker unknown. 96" x 82". Cotton. It is virtually impossible for the eye to assign any of the narrow, elliptical leaf forms to a particular hexagonal surround because all are shared by pattern areas. The side of one is the center of its neighbor, and on and on. At times the quilt looks more like white cloth, symmetrically slashed in circles of six lines to reveal dark areas beneath. The eye never stops searching for the beginning, that point at which to focus on the intricate network of lines to determine whether white triangles on dark cloth or dark six-pointed stars on white predominate. (*Author's collection.*)

3.85

3.86

FIG. 3.86. Double Wedding Ring pattern pieced quilt, Amish, c. 1930, Ohio. Maker unknown. Dimensions unavailable. Cotton. While most examples of the Double Wedding Ring pattern have a circular formation, here the somewhat squared dimension of the rings causes the viewer to perceive bow-knot forms, or four-leaf extensions, caught at their centers with pink and purple squares. Simultaneously, the black concave diamonds surrounded by the touching leaf forms advance as a distinct figural element vying for attention with the multicolor areas. (*Photo courtesy Judi Boisson Antique American Quilts.*)

FIG. 3.87. Double Wedding Ring pattern pieced quilt, Amish, c. 1930, Holmes County, Ohio. Maker unknown. Dimensions unavailable. Cotton. An illusion of never-ending revolution has been created with strips of intensely colored pastels, some of which are so close in value to the hot turquoise field as to dissolve or recede while the ringed fields advance. Classic versions of the Double Wedding Ring pattern, incorporating pretty printed pastels against a white field, are static in comparison with the vitality of this Amish example. (*Photo courtesy Judy Boisson Antique American Quilts.*)

FIG. 3.88. Pickle Dish (Double Wedding Ring variation) pattern pieced quilt, c. 1925, locale unknown. Maker unknown. 75″ square. Cotton. The traditional ring shape has been altered here, leaving the thinnest black ellipse between most of the squared-off curves of the visually interlocking rings. The maker restrained the prints and palette, either alternating light and dark strips or choosing fabrics so close in value that they merge as solid areas. This lovely, painterly illusion reads in places like overlays of transparent shading, sheer here and built to deeper tone there. In areas where the tonal contrasts are greater, those elements advance and fan out as spidery forms. (*Photo courtesy Darwin D. Bearley.*)

Fig. 3.89. Double Wedding Ring pattern pieced quilt, Amish, c. 1940, Holmes County, Ohio. Maker unknown. Dimensions unavailable. Cotton sateen. In this intensely contrasting example, the rings actually appear to be in endless linkage, like a puzzle ring or Romanesque guilloche. They seem to loop through each other, reading both over and under, rather than simply connecting to the four-patch intersection as is characteristic of the Wedding Ring design. This visual phenomenon is caused by the closeness or distance in value of the strips adjoining the intersections. (*Photo courtesy Judi Boisson Antique American Quilts.*)

Fig. 3.90. Wheel of Mysterie pattern pieced quilt, c. 1930. Virginia. Maker unknown. 80″ x 68″. Cotton. Although the main elements of this quilt are curvy triangles set out as four-patch-type blocks, the design's effect is so decidedly curvilinear that the viewer perceives constantly overlapping circles. The structural blocks alternate medium and light tones within and are then arrayed in alternating sequence so that the overall image is of a positive/negative kinetic illusion where shadows of circles keep drawing the viewer in. (*Photo courtesy Stella Rubin.*)

Fig. 3.91. Pincushion pattern pieced quilt, c. 1920, New York. Maker unknown. 76″ x 62″. Cotton. This quilt's maker adapted a very early pieced pattern and updated its impact by coordinating (not quite perfectly) the direction of the strips in the light-colored elliptical areas so that they read as concentric diamonds spreading in succession beneath the black grid. The result is that an almost medieval tracery of attentuated four-pointed stars seems to have been cut from black cloth and placed over a background of pale strips. In addition to the multi-layered effect, the light and dark areas alternate in visual dominance. (*Author's collection.*)

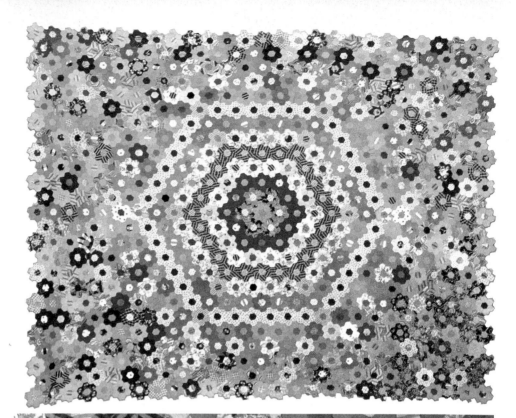

FIGS. 3.92, 3.93. Honeycomb (Mosaic variation) pattern pieced quilt top and detail, c. 1860, Pennsylvania. Maker unknown. 92″ x 76″. Wool challis. To convey the illusion of large hexagons expanding concentrically, the tonalities of the central area of the quilt have been aligned and orchestrated in contrast, just as in the straight-edged examples of figures 1.12 and 3.66. At the outside edges, this tonal contrast has been abandoned in favor of the more classic format, where hexagonal "rosettes" or "cells" appear independently. The lighter groupings pop up from the densely patterned surface; the darker ones recede or even merge and sometimes disappear where the fabrics are close in tone. The detail shows the nickel-sized hexagons organized in their familiar "rosettes" of seven patches (six hexagons surrounding a central hexagon). In it, both the tonal alignment that has created the larger scale dynamic graphic effect, and the tonal diffusion that has produced random effects of light and dark upon the retina, are revealed. (*Author's collection.*)

FIG. 3.94. Hexagon (Crazy Quilt variation) pattern pieced quilt, dated 1886, locale unknown. Signed "To Louise from Grandma Crory." Dimensions unavailable. Silk and velvet. Nearly kaleidoscopic hexagons in shimmering gold, beige, and rose advance and recede in relation to the surrounding black hexagonal forms. These dark elements unite as trilobed forms, pointing up or down, lying over or under, the lighter hexagonally shaped areas. As in a crazy quilt, the pattern pieces are imprecisely aligned by size and shape, yet the result reads as multiple hexagons in the viewer's perception. (*Photo courtesy Judi Boisson Antique American Quilts.*)

FIG. 3.95. Mosaic (Hexagon variation) pattern pieced quilt, c. 1890, locale unknown. Maker unknown. Dimensions unavailable. Cotton. This micromosaic composition looks as if it has been photographed with a depth-of-field distortion that cause pale "dots" to float up from the crowded quilt surface. The darkest and lightest shades advance from a field of thousands of hexagons because of the specific optical interaction of their contrasting tones with the retina of the eye. (*Photo courtesy Darwin D. Bearley.*)

Figs. 3.96, 3.97. Milky Way pattern pieced quilt and detail, c. 1870, Whitlock, Tennessee. 84" x 71". Cotton. In this rarely seen composition, dark hexagonal sections appear simultaneously as distinct elements on a patterned background and as the background of an intricate six-pointed star made from Log Cabin strips. Executing this design to achieve a consistent result required skillful attention to the length of the strips and the placement of the fabrics. As the detail illustrates, the quilt has been cut and pieced like a Log Cabin Windmill Blades variation, with the diagonally clipped strip ends arranged around a dark "hearth." (Collection of Brenda F. Fuller; photo courtesy Quilts of Tennessee.)

Fig. 3.98. Star Medallion pattern pieced quilt, Amish, c. 1910, Elkhart, Indiana. Maker unknown. 77″ x 73″. Cotton. Similar in construction to the Tumbling Blocks pattern (figs. 3.49 and 4.2), this harmonious composition reads like an illuminated field of stars. The eye simultaneously perceives black stars advancing from a pale field, while light-colored hexagonal dots drift up from a dark surface. This continual shift in perception makes for an intriguing, rich composition. (*Photo courtesy Judi Boisson Antique American Quilts.*)

Fig. 3.99. Honeycomb (Mosaic variation) pattern pieced quilt, c. 1880, Henry County, Kentucky. Made by Sophronia Ann Bruce. 107″ x 92″. Cotton, wool, and silk. The configuration of this unique ten-pointed star is so complex and atypical that it seems more like an architectural rendering of a three-dimensional star that has been dissected for inspection than a quilting motif. The rosettes or concentric hexagonal "cells" traditionally arrayed in an allover pattern most familiar as Grandmother's Flower Garden take on unusual dimension here. The maker seems to have attempted a "tinker toy" construction in this grand-scale image, and in the process has conveyed a spatial illusion of breadth and shallow depth. The resulting bedcover, certainly kept as a "best" quilt rather than used on a daily basis, has true three-dimensionality, for the field is filled with elaborate stuffed work and padding. (*Photo courtesy Kentucky Quilt Project.*)

Combinations, Representational Forms, and Eccentric Designs

THE QUILTS ILLUSTRATED IN THIS SECTION include examples in which two or more distinct geometric shapes are joined in the pattern blocks—thus qualifying them as combinations. Also shown are quilts whose patterns combine two or more different pieced blocks to develop an interlocking, graphic, and illusionary composition.

The representational forms include images such as a flower, a tree, or other clearly pictorial elements. These are among the least common forms of illusion, because even though they may have been pared down to their essential geometric bases in the manner of abstract art suggestive of naturalistic elements, they will still read as pictorial images unless some form of block rotation is used. For example, the Tree of Life quilt illustrated in Chapter 4 (fig. 4.4) looks nothing like that classic pattern until the viewer can locate its primary block. By rotating the blocks so that the angled elements abut, the Tree of Life quilt's maker created a large-scale, dynamic graphic whole that completely subordinates the pictorial image to geometric illusionary forms.

The eccentric examples given here are so unusual and out of the ordinary that they defy ready categorization. The Depression-era Target quilt (fig. 3.112), for example, is a highly original composition whose inspiration appears to have come from no readily identifiable source. The compelling graphics of the much earlier Diamond in a Square variation (fig. 3.113) are alive with movement.

FIG. 3.100. Touching Stars (Crazy Quilt variation) pattern pieced quilt, dated 1896, Schoeneck, Lancaster County, Pennsylvania. Made by Lizzie Rock Edwards. 81" x 80". Wool. Two distinct geometric designs —a series of two- and four-patch blocks, along with a series of octagonal spoked wheels—seem to float on a field embellished with Victorian embroidery stitches. In reality the field is the quilt's primary structure, a format of touching eight-pointed stars. The random, mostly tetrahedral-shaped patches that form the arms seem to submerge in competition with the solid-color blocks. The network of intricate stitchery is so like an overlay that it obscures the piecing beneath. Wheels emerge from the triangular centers of the stars because they are outlined and embroidered. It is remarkable to find this intricacy and delicacy in wool in an era in which such piecing and needlework would usually have been reserved for silk. (*Photo courtesy M. Finkel & Daughter.*)

3.101

3.102

Fig. 3.101. Foundation Rose and Pine Tree pattern appliqué quilt, c. 1915, Ohio. Maker unknown. 70″ square. Cotton. Floral appliqué quilts with illusionary qualities are rare, particularly when striking geometric forms arise from the precise appliqué work. This example reads more like interlocking circles and four-pointed stars than the blossoms and clusters of pine trees which were the quiltmaker's intention to depict in fabric. Its nine repeat blocks were organized so that the points of the conical trees nearly touch, drawing the viewer's attention from the blossom centers to the other emergent designs. The appliqué block here is similar to figure 1.23, but it conveys different graphic impressions because of the relative areas between pattern and field. (*Photo courtesy Darwin D. Bearley.*)

Fig. 3.102. Cockscomb and Currants pattern appliqué quilt, c. 1880, Pennsylvania. Maker unknown. 78″ x 76″. Cotton. The close juxtaposition of the appliqué elements has transformed the field into a prominent design element which competes for attention with the representational motifs. The near union of the extended elements of leaves, currants, and blossom tips has created an illusion which outlines a square element of appliqué and a cruciform bordered with inwardly curving leaves. Both field and pattern advance and recede as the eye shifts focus, revealing how the abstraction of a naturalistic form generates unanticipated geometric designs. (*Author's collection.*)

Fig. 3.103. Spice Pink pattern appliqué quilt, c. 1870, Tennessee. Made by Mary Adams Heaton. 103¾″ x 85¼″. Cotton. A sprightly, delicate allover geometric surface has been fashioned through the repetition of thirty floral appliqué blocks. The slender stems which join buds to blossoms consequently outline varied geometric forms in white. The phenomenon of closure oper-

3.103

ates here as in other designs where elongated pattern elements "touch," causing imaginary linkages in ways the quilter probably never could have conceived. (*Photo courtesy Quilts of Tennessee.*)

FIG. 3.104. Spider's Web pattern pieced quilt, Mennonite (Horse and Buggy Sect), c. 1920, Ohio. Maker unknown. 82″ x 74″. Wool. Each square pattern block creates an illusion within itself, as well as larger and dif-

ferent illusions when the blocks are linked. Eight elongated triangles composed of wool strips of deeply saturated solid hues comprise each block. Every other triangle bears an identical color se-

quence of strips, from which the viewer perceives four-arm windmill-like geometrics that pulsate above striped octagons which appear through the illusion of closure. (*Collection of M. Finkel & Daughter.*)

3.105

3.106

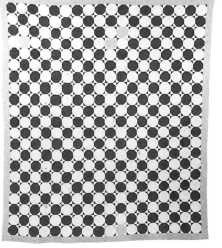

3.107

FIG. 3.105. Arabic Lattice pattern pieced quilt, dated 1931, Ohio. Maker unknown. 70″ square. Cotton. In this rarely attempted pattern, the pointed elements, like perky caps, convey a sense of rollicking motion. The figure/ground illusion switches back and forth in the viewer's perception between the identical light and dark shapes. As in its optical counterpart, the Indiana Puzzle (figs. 1.4 and 3.115), the diamond-shaped pattern pieces are here linked with tiny four-patch segments that visually entwine the figures and delightfully distort perception. (*Collection of Michael Council.*)

FIG. 3.106. Bowknot (Farmer's Puzzle variation) pattern pieced quilt, c. 1910, Fayetteville, Tennessee. Made by the Ladies' Missionary Society of the Cumberland Presbyterian Church. 78″ square. Cotton. Lines that sizzle like a cartoonist's rendition of radio waves draw simultaneous attention to the images of a four-pointed star caught at each corner by a rosette and of a fleur-de-lis centered with a rosette. The angles imply constant tension and motion in this simple yet effective composition of dark strips with white triangles and diamonds. (*Collection of Michelle Johnson Rowe; photo courtesy Quilts of Tennessee.*)

FIG. 3.107. Robbing Peter to Pay Paul pattern pieced quilt, c. 1915, Ohio. Maker unknown. 80″ x 76″. Cotton. A checkerboard-like surface of apparent dots vies with the actual composition of tiny Broken Dishes blocks and larger solid areas. These patches, when joined with the diagonal sides of the solids, create the illusion of circular rather than angular shapes through the phenomenon of closure: the mind perceives curves where none exist. In addition, the small-scale patches seem to merge and disappear as background as the dots surface in our view. (*Photo courtesy Darwin D. Bearley.*)

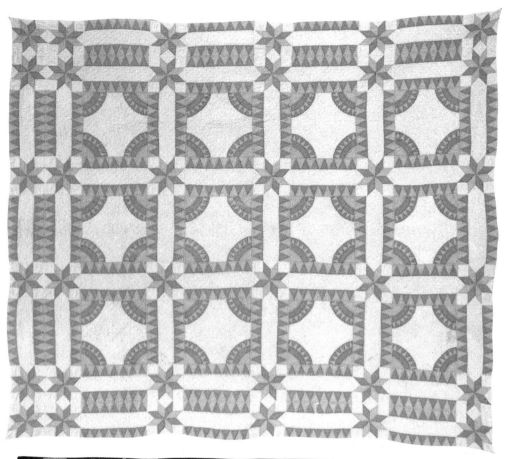

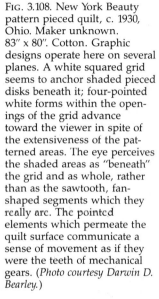

Fig. 3.108. New York Beauty pattern pieced quilt, c. 1930, Ohio. Maker unknown. 83″ x 80″. Cotton. Graphic designs operate here on several planes. A white squared grid seems to anchor shaded pieced disks beneath it; four-pointed white forms within the openings of the grid advance toward the viewer in spite of the extensiveness of the patterned areas. The eye perceives the shaded areas as "beneath" the grid and as whole, rather than as the sawtooth, fan-shaped segments which they really are. The pointed elements which permeate the quilt surface communicate a sense of movement as if they were the teeth of mechanical gears. (*Photo courtesy Darwin D. Bearley.*)

Fig. 3.109 Steeplechase pattern pieced quilt, dated 1883, Brooklyn, New York. Inscribed on back "Made by Old Ladies in the Old Ladies Home." 55″ x 41″. Cotton. In this aptly named design the eye cannot chose what to focus on. Darks and lights race on the diagonal; strongly contrasting squared circles (or are they curvilinear squares?) seem to arise from the kinetic surroundings in this two-tone composition of triangular and arrow-like forms. This intriguing confusion is known as a figure/ground illusion. (*Collection of Paula Laverty.*)

FIG. 3.110. Rabbit's Paw (Goose in the Pond variation) pattern pieced quilt, Amish, dated Jan. 22, 1930, Middlebury, Indiana. Made by Mrs. Amanda Yoder. Initialed "J.D.F." 55" x 48". Cotton. One dozen red and blue pieced blocks have been joined with intersecting blocks of red eight-pointed stars to convey a larger interconnected pattern. The eye shifts between the pattern block and its link. Because of the similarity in color between paw and star, fiery hot X-shaped "brands" appear to hold the paw blocks in place. Their radiant glow is so intense as to read like the absence of color, making the blue areas advance as if transparent above the red squares. (*Photo courtesy Esprit Quilt Collection.*)

FIG. 3.111. Tulip Bud pattern appliqué quilt, c. 1915, Ohio. Maker unknown. 80" x 75". Cotton. Blocks of four yellow tulip buds set with their bases pointed inward toward a center square are repeated thirty times without separation, becoming an abstract geometric design. The tulips almost disappear as the eye perceives a cross set within four-pointed concave stars set within a circular framework. The cross and star designs share elliptical sides with the neighboring blocks, an effect similar to figure 1.21 (Robbing Peter to Pay Paul). The structural block is identifiable if the surface is read from a corner within the pale inner border, showing how each block lends a bud to the overall curvilinear effect. (*Photo courtesy Darwin D. Bearley.*)

FIG. 3.112. Target (Quill variation) pattern pieced quilt, c. 1930, Kentucky. Made by Hattie McWilliams. 86″ x 76″. Rayon and cotton. This Afro-American bedcover is the only quilt in this book whose entire surface is actually three-dimensional. Its fundamental illusion, however, comes from the manipulation of color rather than layering. Thousands of one inch "prairie points" or "porcupine quills" (the folded triangles of fabric which are the patches) combine in a scheme of great drama and energy. The central image of a vortex or comet draws the eye in, while the rays of light and dark extending from that oval area simultaneously direct the eye beyond the quilt's borders. The tactile surface results from sewing the points only at their bases, leaving the tips free to overlap the previous rows. The points face inward and are aligned by color to enhance the sense of a tumultuous vortex. (*Author's collection.*)

FIG. 3.113. Unnamed pattern (Diamond in a Square variation) pieced quilt top, c. 1875, Massachusetts. Maker unknown. 90½″ square. Cotton and chintz. This stunning graphic knockout is unique in its organization of small squares, strips, and triangles. Activity is suggested on many planes—in the foreground and background, at the center, and bursting out to the sides. An array of points, diagonals, and interrupted borders leads the eye deep into and out of the flat surface. The quilt's explosive imagery is reminiscent of Op Art, but its execution predates that art movement by nearly a century. A refined palette of solid, warm earth tones and mauves has here become a work of art daring for its era. (*Collection Museum of American Folk Art; gift of Cyril I. Nelson.*)

3.114

FIG. 3.114. Lily pattern pieced quilt, c. 1865, Trigg County, Kentucky. Made by a member of either the Burgess or Stewart family. 88″ x 72″. Cotton. The stylization of the flower heads, and their arrangement in a group of three whose stems touch, generate a design in which realistic representation takes a back seat to the illusion of a composition of triangles and six-pointed stars. Even though the quilt is pieced of twenty-eight full- and eight half-lily blocks, triangles seem to be outlined by the sashing and are prominent in the field surrounding the lily clusters. (*Photo courtesy The Kentucky Quilt Project.*)

3.115

FIG. 3.115. Indiana Puzzle pattern pieced quilt, c. 1920, Ohio. Maker unknown. 78″ x 74″. Cotton. Intertwined forms mirror each other in this positive/negative figure/ground illusion. The reversible imagery is related to figure 1.4, but here the figures have been elongated and exaggerated in their curvilinear interconnectedness by the three different geometric patches that corner the squares. This rolling graphic resembles the textile designs by Kolomon Moser for the Wiener Werkstätte, which were becoming known at about the time this quilt was made. (*Author's collection.*)

FIG. 3.116. Fly Foot pattern pieced quilt top, Amish, c. 1880, Belleville, Pennsylvania. Maker unknown. 72″ x 69″. Wool. Square blocks in two colors (red and black), bisected either vertically or diagonally, are alternated to create a design of positive/negative illusion. From one perspective, large, skewed, dark X's shift in and out of view; from the other, a network of shaded alternating brickwork dominates. (*Author's collection.*)

3.116

FIG. 3.117. Double Hearts pattern appliqué quilt, c. 1935, Missouri. Maker unknown. 92″ x 90″. Cotton. This unique appliqué uses geometrics rather than florals to achieve an optical illusion that is totally reversible in impact. A dark clover-like element, composed of four hearts whose bases point in toward each other, vies for attention with a starry eight-pointed white element. United, the darks form a horizontal/vertical grid, while the attenuated diagonal points of the white elements unite to form an attention-getting diagonal grid. The eye constantly shifts between the two strong designs. (*Collection of The Fosters.*)

3.117

3.118

FIGS. 3.118, 3.119. Chimney Sweep pattern pieced quilt and detail, c. 1940, Vonore, Tennessee. Made by Lois Hall. 87" x 67". Cotton. X marks the spot, or, more precisely, the block from which this multi-layered kaleidoscopic design emerges. The crisscross form employs one cotton print per block, united by a white center diamond. By adding two black diamonds within the print's right angles, the quiltmaker perhaps unwittingly created a bold, black octagonal grid beneath the light print latticework grid. Where the print and black are closest in color, splashy dark clusters seem to pop out from a pastel field. Diagonals, points, and tonal contrast convey a strong sense of movement by perceptually linking up grids. (*Collection of Lois Hall; photo courtesy Quilts of Tennessee.*)

3.119

3.120

FIG. 3.120. Hayes' Corner pattern pieced quilt, Amish, c. 1925, Mifflin County, Pennsylvania. Maker unknown. 80" x 75". Cotton. Concentric diamonds and an overlying yet seemingly transparent grid emerge from this simple nine-patch variation of squares and triangles. The whole composition seems the reverse of what we would expect to see. A boldly contrasting diagonal image should dominate the surface, as in the Log Cabin Barn Raising variation, rather than operating as if beneath a lighter visual element. This spatial illusion extends even to the quilt's borders, where we imagine that the outermost diamonds become complete. (*Photo courtesy Darwin D. Bearley.*)

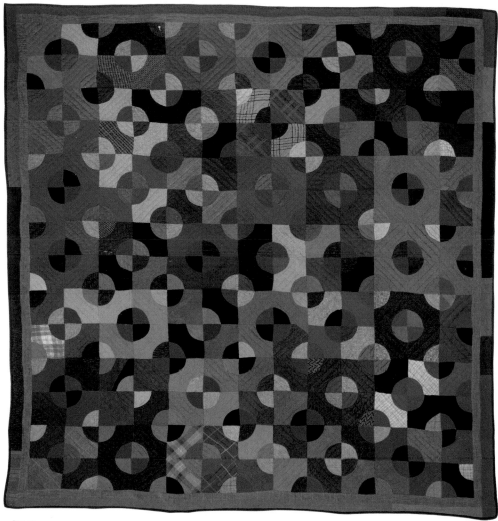

FIG. 3.121. Mill Wheel (Steeplechase variation) pattern pieced quilt, Mennonite, c. 1890, Ohio. Maker unknown. 74" square. Wool. Depending upon the juxtaposition of colors alone, whole and quartered dots appear to float above solid or fragmented blocks in this intriguing composition. In reality, the construction is based on small squares from which quarter circles have been cut on opposing corners. The vacant quarter circles are then pieced in with different colors. When four blocks are joined with these quarter circles abutting, circles of contrasting or complementary colors result. This masterpiece, made from suiting scraps, is similar to the broken overlapping circles present in twentieth-century works by Frank Stella and Sonia Delaunay. (*Author's collection.*)

FIG. 3.122. New York Beauty pattern pieced quilt, c. 1930, West Virginia. Maker unknown. 80" x 75". Cotton. This exuberant version of an always bold graphic design features elements that appear to spin gaily throughout a densely patterned surface. The grid-over-circles illusion in typical variations of the New York Beauty pattern is here almost subordinated by star bursts that sometimes appear through the tonal proximity of patches to the white field. Adding a folksy appeal to an often formal composition, these accidental stars go off in every direction, while the fan shapes merge like a patterned ground. (*Photo courtesy Darwin D. Bearley.*)

4.

HOW TO CREATE QUILTS OF ILLUSION

t is probably safe to say that no quiltmaker ever lacks challenges: most probably have more ideas waiting to be translated into cloth than there is ever time—or fabric enough—to complete. However, on the theory that readers of *Quilts of Illusion* may wish to attempt some of their own illusionary designs, this chapter features a quartet of traditional patterns—Eccentric Star, Tumbling Blocks, Three-Dimensional Fans (a Tumbling Blocks variation), and Tree of Life—that are anything *but* traditional in execution.

Full-size templates, piecing diagrams, and step-by-step instructions accompany large full-color photographs of each original quilt. Fabric requirements are given for two of the quilts (Eccentric Star and Tree of Life); the other two, because of the number of different fabrics used in their execution, are classified as scrap quilts, making estimates of yardage both difficult and unnecessary. (Either Tumbling Blocks quilt would provide an ideal opportunity for a quilter to utilize the fabric leftovers hoarded for just the right occasion.)

Whether you attempt to reproduce one of these superb bedcovers exactly or use it as a point of departure to create your own contemporary masterpiece is up to you. For instance, it might be interesting to experiment with a block quilt other than the Tree of Life illustrated in figure 4.4. A Log Cabin, a Drunkard's Path, or one of the other block quilts illustrated in Chapter 3 might provide inspiration. If you do choose to attempt your own unique illusion, you might want to begin with a pen and a paper, rather than a needle and thread. By drawing one representative block, photocopying it numerous times, and laying out the copies in various arrangements, you'll arrive at an overall pattern that creates the illusion you're trying to achieve. If you have the time and patience, using colored paper to form multiple blocks will give you an even better idea of what the end results will be. Your choice of fabric colors will be all-important: as is evident from many of the quilts illustrated in this book, color plays a major role in creating optical illusions.

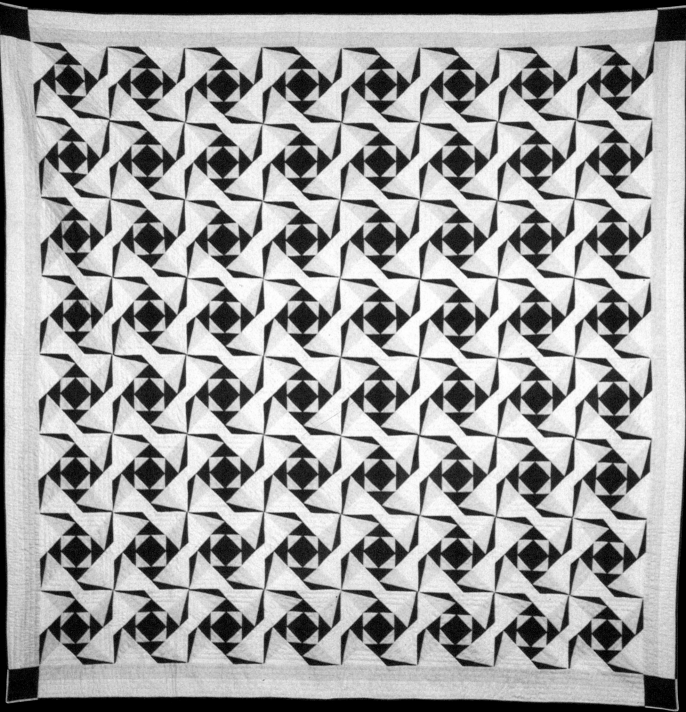

Eccentric Star

BECAUSE THE MAKER of this particular Eccentric Star quilt restricted her palette to three colors, two of which—the yellow and the off-white—give little contrast, the optical illusions that result from the pattern are more subtle than they would have been had more vibrantly colored fabrics been chosen. Sixty-four identical blocks, each 8½″ square, comprise the basic quilt. Each block is composed of six basic pattern pieces—five triangles and a square. While the individual blocks may look complicated to piece, each separate template uses only one color of fabric. Therefore the cutting of the shapes is basically quite a simple procedure, so long as normal care is taken to insure that each piece is accurately measured and cut (add ¼″ seam allowance for each template).

Once you have prepared sufficient pieces for the number of blocks you've decided upon for the quilt, begin the piecing of each block from the center, stitching the four (yellow) triangles to the central red square (thus making a larger square). Then piece the four triangles that make up each side of the outer block, stitching them in turn to the inner square. Once all of the blocks are sewn, it's a simple matter to pin and stitch them together in straight rows, affixing each row to the one above until the main design is completed.

This particular quilt is bordered with strips of the yellow and off-white fabric interrupted at each corner with a red square (twice the width of the strips), the whole rimmed with a contrasting narrow border of red (yellow where the narrow border abuts the outer red squares). You might choose a border of another width, or one pieced of a single color, for a different look.

Fabric requirements (without border or backing): You'll need 2¾ yards of the red fabric, 2¼ yards of the yellow, and 1½ yards of the off-white to complete a quilt of equal size (based on using fabrics that are 45″ wide).

FIG. 4.1. Eccentric Star pattern pieced quilt, c. 1930, Ohio. Maker unknown. 78″ square. Cotton. Although generally considered a star pattern, this complex design appears to combine the Diamond-in-a-Square and Pinwheel patterns. Where the two patterns meet, wispy white Fly Foot shapes emerge to veil the entire composition. Each element seems to twist and extend into the neighboring segment. Even the white "negative" space around the pieced red and yellow areas becomes a distinct geometric shape. (*Author's collection.*)

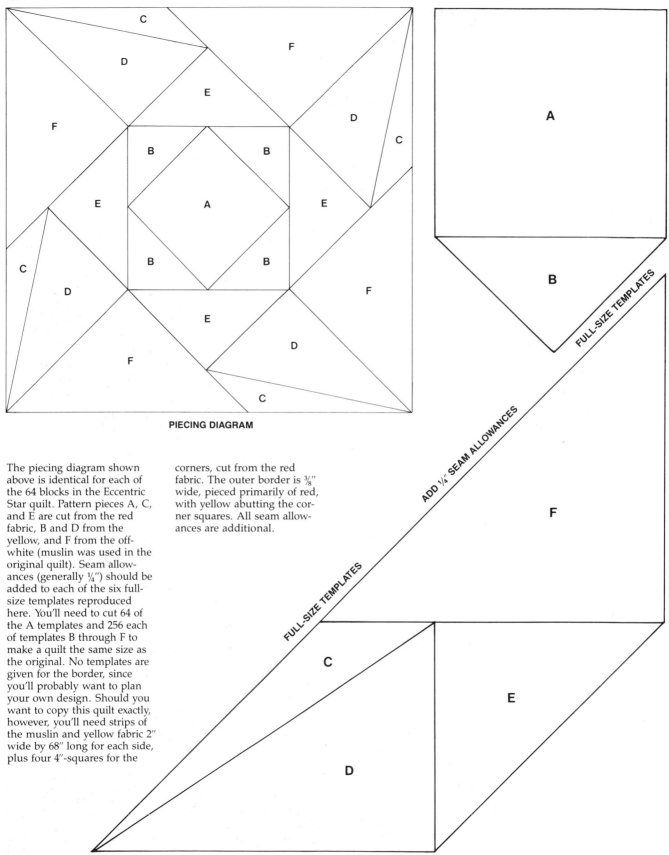

PIECING DIAGRAM

FULL-SIZE TEMPLATES

ADD ¼″ SEAM ALLOWANCES

FULL-SIZE TEMPLATES

The piecing diagram shown above is identical for each of the 64 blocks in the Eccentric Star quilt. Pattern pieces A, C, and E are cut from the red fabric, B and D from the yellow, and F from the off-white (muslin was used in the original quilt). Seam allowances (generally ¼″) should be added to each of the six full-size templates reproduced here. You'll need to cut 64 of the A templates and 256 each of templates B through F to make a quilt the same size as the original. No templates are given for the border, since you'll probably want to plan your own design. Should you want to copy this quilt exactly, however, you'll need strips of the muslin and yellow fabric 2″ wide by 68″ long for each side, plus four 4″-squares for the corners, cut from the red fabric. The outer border is ⅜″ wide, pieced primarily of red, with yellow abutting the corner squares. All seam allowances are additional.

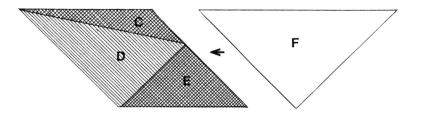

Begin each block by piecing the four B triangles to the central A square. When this is completed, you'll have formed another larger square in which the center has been rotated to become a diamond.

The trapezoids formed of the C, D, E, and F templates are next sewn, in turn, to the central diamond-in-a-square formed of the A and B pieces.

Begin at the top and move in a clockwise direction, using great care in the joining of the final trapezoid. (See piecing diagram, below.)

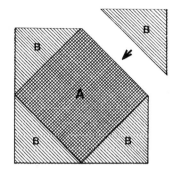

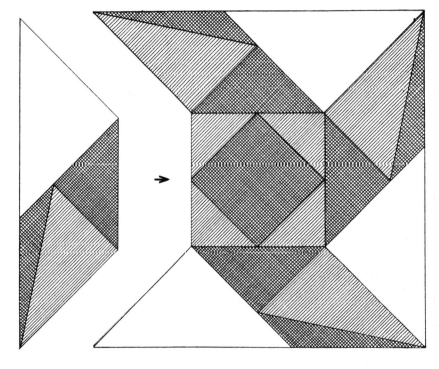

Piece the outer triangles of the block: C to D, then E to D (as shown below) and, finally, F to the diagonal formed by the C, D, and E triangles (see piecing diagram, upper right). Once you have repeated this step four times, you'll have four identical trapezoids.

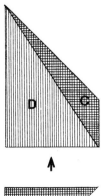

Once you have completed the sewing of all blocks necessary to complete the quilt, carefully pin one block to the next, and sew each in turn until you have a row of eight completed (either horizontally or vertically, as you prefer). Once each row is completed, it will be a relatively easy matter to pin and sew each row to the next until all 64 blocks are joined. The border, batting, and backing are left to your discretion. If you prefer a larger quilt than this, you can add additional blocks to both the horizontal and vertical rows until a desired size is achieved.

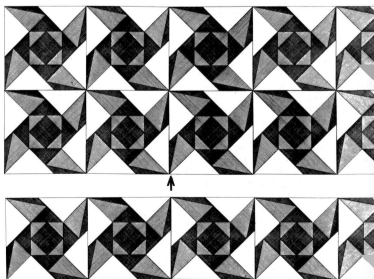

Tumbling Blocks (Seven Sisters Variation)

THIS DAZZLING COMPOSITION, pieced of a wide variety of silk and velvet prints and solids, may at first appear to be a scrap quilt, its basic tumbling blocks or cubes arranged with no attention to the optical illusions that result when they are stitched together. And in terms of the sheer numbers of fabrics employed, it could be classified as such. More careful study of the placement of the diamonds that form each cube, however, shows that the quilter did have a scheme in mind. Most of the cubes were planned in groups of three (in a rough upside-down Y shape), with careful attention given to the arrangement of equal numbers of light, medium, and dark fabric pieces. The majority of the three-block groups were sewn with identical dark fabrics always placed on the outer edges of the cubes and light and medium fabrics alternated to form a six-pointed star when the three blocks were joined. The result, depending upon the brightness of the fabrics used for each trio of blocks, is that in some areas the six-pointed stars are prominent, while in others the lightest of the three fabrics used for the trio forms a dominant three-pointed form.

To emulate the intricate illusions present in the original quilt, the modern needleworker will probably want to cut and piece most of the block trios before beginning to sew the elements together. Those basic elements can then be arranged in various configurations until the desired effect is achieved.

While the original quilt has no border (the edges appear to have been clipped, folded under, and sewn to the backing), a solid-color frame might be effective in containing the exuberance of this blinding composition. Anything other than a solid color, however, would serve only to add confusion to the design.

FIG. 4.2 Tumbling Blocks (Seven Sisters variation) pattern pieced quilt, c. 1880, Ohio. Maker unknown. 68" x 54". Silk and velvet. Because of the quilter's attention to the juxtaposition of light, medium, and dark fabrics in the piecing of each cube, together with the light-reflecting properties of the luxurious silks and velvets she used, a variety of geometric forms appears. Among the shapes visible in this vibrant quilt (in addition to the blocks one would normally expect to see) are light and dark hexagons, six-pointed stars, and pale three-pronged elements. It is interesting to compare this mysterious composition with some of the more straightforward Tumbling Blocks quilts illustrated in Chapter 3. (*Author's collection.*)

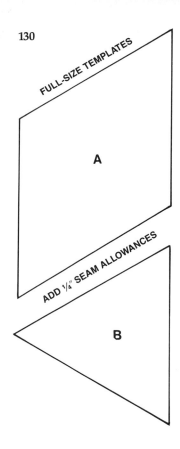

FULL-SIZE TEMPLATES

A

ADD ¼" SEAM ALLOWANCES

B

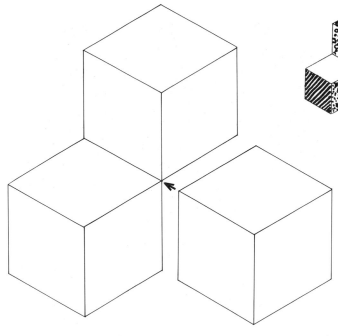

Working in groups of three, join cubes in an inverted Y shape, with the dark fabrics on the outside and the medium and light ones alternated as shown in the piecing diagram below. You'll want to make a majority of the trios in this fashion, using identical light, medium, and dark fabrics for each cube in the threesome, but reserve some odd fabrics for "eccentric" arrangements as shown at the upper right.

Once you've completed enough of the inverted Y's to make a quilt of the size you've chosen (this quilt contains 9 of the trios in width and 11 in length, for a total of 99), try different arrangements until you've arrived at a configuration that gives you the illusions you want. Then number each trio of cubes on the back, from top to bottom. Begin piecing a center vertical strip, as shown.

Three identical diamonds (template A) form each full cube in this Seven Sisters variation. The triangle (B) is used to fill in the sides once the rest of the quilt has been pieced.

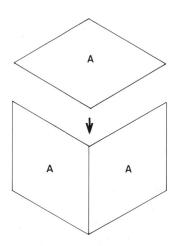

A

A   A

Piece each cube by joining three of the A diamonds as shown, using a different fabric for each diamond. Each cube should contain a light, medium, and dark fabric.

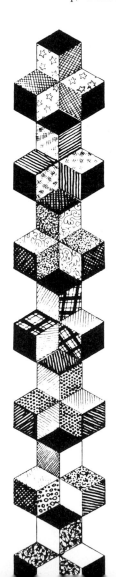

Once the central strip is completed, add a row to each side, one trio of cubes at a time, until the bulk of the quilt is completed. (Joining the pieces in this fashion avoids the sewing of difficult right angles.) To finish the top and bottom of the quilt, add double and single cubes, respectively.

To complete the sides, you'll need to make a certain number of wedge-shaped pieces, using one each of the A and B templates. Cut them as mirror images (see the piecing diagram below) and fit in where needed. When you attach the quilt top to the backing, fold over the serrated edges of the top and bottom and pin, then stitch. (You might wish to add a solid border, although this particular quilt does not have one.)

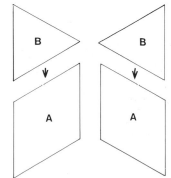

Three-Dimensional Fans

An INGENIOUS VARIATION of a basic Tumbling Blocks pattern, as is the Seven Sisters quilt shown in figure 4.2, this Three-Dimensional Fans quilt has been intricately pieced of rich silks and velvets. The top of each block—a square, rather than a diamond as in the previous quilt—has been divided into nine pieces to simulate a lady's fan. The profusion of fabrics used in the piecing qualifies this as a scrap quilt. Yet the quilter has arranged the variety of fabrics in a somewhat regimented way. Black velvet forms the base of each fan. The odd-shaped strips connected to the bases are pieced of just two fabrics—one light and one dark—carefully alternated to achieve contrast. The bases of the blocks are always composed of fabrics of contrasting shades. While there is no fixed pattern to the placement of the lighter or darker fabrics, the majority of the darker ones seem to be positioned on the right.

The preliminary cutting and piecing of each block is much more complicated than that of the Seven Sisters block because of the eight wedges that form the top of each fan and the curved piece that forms the base. However, once each block is completed (there are a total of 196 blocks in this composition—14 down and 14 across), they are joined in much the same way as the block trios of the Seven Sisters pattern. A vertical row is sewn together, and individual blocks are attached to each side of it, averting the necessity of piecing right angles.

The border of this unusual quilt is composed of a complex design of velvet triangles and elongated diamonds. The shape of the pieces bears little relation to the quilt's basic design and, in fact, it is obvious that the pieces rounding the corners had to be altered to fit—probably as the top was being completed. Because of the difficulty inherent in trying to size these pieces properly before the quilt top is pieced, no templates are included for the border. It would be far simpler to estimate the number of diamonds and triangles needed once the basic design is completed. The pale green satin backing of this particular quilt creates an outer frame, as the border is sewn to it. A less confusing border might be a better choice.

The finished bedcover is not quilted, but tied with the black silk bows that accent each fan.

FIG. 4.3. Three-Dimensional Fans pattern pieced quilt, c. 1880, Maryland. Maker unknown. 80" x 70". Silk and velvet. The three-dimensional illusion of this Victorian fantasy has been accentuated by transforming the uppermost side of each cube into a miniature fan. Each fan has a base of black velvet tied with a black silk bow; the curve of each base has been embroidered with gold thread. By varying one or two elements of a familiar design, an imaginative quilter can become a pop artist, repeating images dozens of times across a quilt canvas. (*Collection of Marcia Berman and Paul Berberian.*)

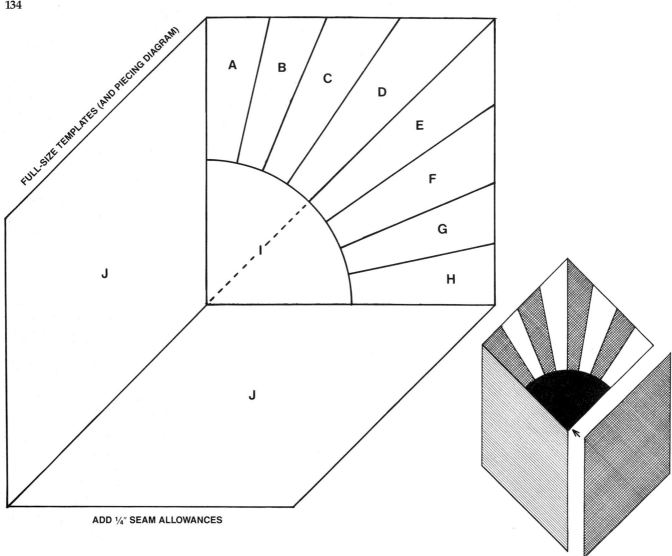

FULL-SIZE TEMPLATES (AND PIECING DIAGRAM)

A B C D E F G H

J

J

I

ADD ¼" SEAM ALLOWANCES

To assemble each full cube, begin by pinning and sewing pieces A through D in sequence, then attach pieces E through H, and join the two sections together as shown

below. Then carefully pin and sew the base of the fan (I) to the top. The cube is completed by sewing each J piece to the fan top (see piecing diagram, upper right).

Assuming that you intend to make a quilt of the same size as the Three-Dimensional Fans example illustrated in figure 4.3, you'll need enough scraps of fabric to complete 196 full cubes. In addition, you'll want to make 15 additional fan tops (templates A to H of the piecing diagram) to be fitted into the bottom of the quilt, and 14 half-cubes split vertically (see dotted line in the diagram). Half of these demi-cubes should be made of templates A to D and J; half of E to H and J. The former will be fitted in to the right side of the quilt; the latter, to the left.

Once all cubes are completed, join a vertical row as shown (opposite page, left). The last piece to be added should be the fan top at the bottom. Add to that first (center) row by filling in the indentations to the left and right in a zigzag pattern.

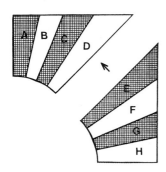

As you reach the bottom of each row, complete it by attaching one of the fan tops (a much simpler procedure than trying to insert them later, which would require sewing right angles). When all rows are completed, fill in the remaining wedges on the left and right sides of the quilt top with half cubes (you'll want 7 for each side). Fold the tops and bottoms, pin, and stitch to the backing in the usual manner.

If you wish to emulate the embroidery used to set off each fan's base, it would be simpler to do so before piecing the quilt. Because of the complicated pattern and the many colors and prints used in the original quilt, the maker chose not to quilt the finished top, but rather tied it with black silk bows that set off the base of each fan.

Tree of Life

THE TREE OF LIFE PATTERN is a familiar representative design that appears often in antique quilts. It suggests pioneer settlement, the importance of the home, and protection. The Tree of Life, or pine tree, is an historic American symbol, seen in flags, coverlets, and political ephemera. As interpreted in this particular quilt, however, it becomes a strong, abstract geometric statement.

Because of the innovative placement of each tree within its block, this quilt appears to be extremely complicated to piece. And because each block is composed of roughly a hundred separate elements, it certainly is not a pattern that a beginner will want to attempt. But once each identical block is dissected and the steps used in the piecing become clear, the task is not as dizzying as it might seem at first glance. Since the quilt utilizes only two fabrics, the job of cutting and piecing is made that much simpler.

Of the 101 pieces in each block, 88 are identical right-angle triangles, 48 cut from the colored (red plaid) fabric, and 40, from muslin. As a first step, 80 of these triangles are joined to make two-toned squares, then the squares attached in rows of increasing length (each row adds one full square) to form the treetops. The balance of the block (the red trunk of the tree and the white background) is composed of larger geometric pieces. If the quilter breaks the basic piecing of each block into three manageable parts, as the piecing diagrams indicate, she should have little trouble in completing each one.

Each horizontal row of six blocks is then sewn in identical fashion, beginning at the left with a block whose treetop is slanted to the upper right, then adding one with the tree turned to the upper left, then right, and so forth until six blocks are joined. Each of the seven horizontal rows is sewn in this manner, then every other row is inverted so that the trees are upside down.

The simple border of this Tree of Life quilt is a ⅜″ binding of the red plain fabric which helps to contain the labyrinthine pattern. Not so simple is the quilting design—a complex combination of diamonds and leaves.

Fabric requirements (without border or backing): You'll need 2⅓ yards of the red fabric, and 3 yards of the muslin (predicated on using 45″-wide fabric in both cases).

FIG. 4.4. Tree of Life pattern pieced quilt, c. 1890, probably Pennsylvania. Maker unknown. 80″ x 68″. Cotton. In the usual Tree of Life pattern, the quilter would align the trees in straight rows within their blocks, giving them the appearance they would have in the natural environment. In this rare example, each tree has been placed on the diagonal within its block, and the blocks positioned in groups of four so that they "touch" at the treetops, creating startling graphic designs. The result of this artistic innovation is a group of geometric motifs that mask the representational aspect of the quilt. The trickery is heightened by the needleworker's choice of a red-and-black buffalo plaid as one of the two fabrics used for the design. (*Author's collection.*)

138

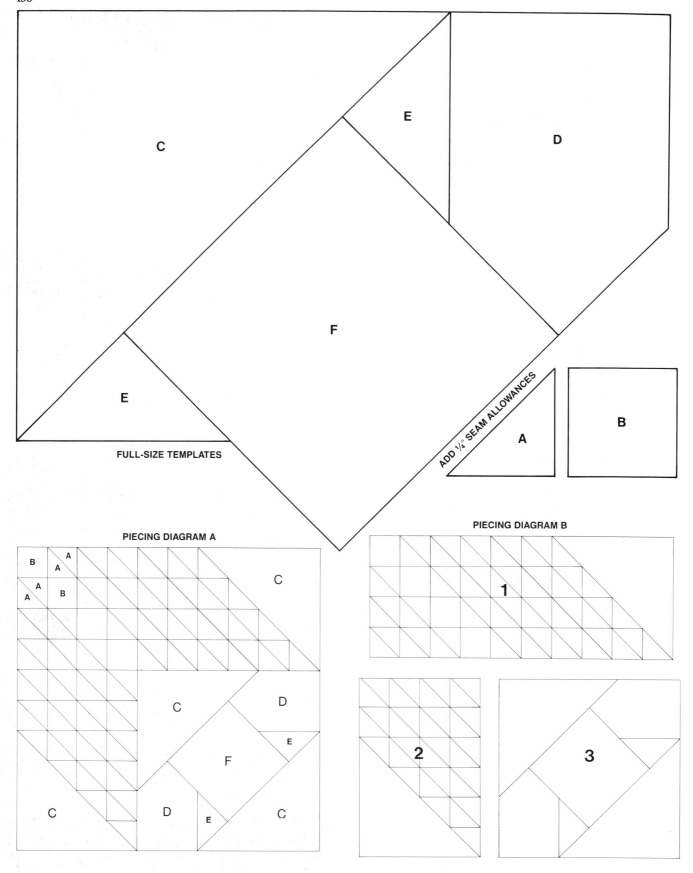

C

E

D

E

F

ADD ¼" SEAM ALLOWANCES

A

B

FULL-SIZE TEMPLATES

PIECING DIAGRAM A

B   A
    A
A   B   C
A

C   D

E

F

C   D   E   C

PIECING DIAGRAM B

1

2   3

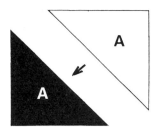

Using template A, cut 88 triangles for each block—48 of the red fabric and 40 of the muslin. Stitch 40 squares using one triangle of each fabric.

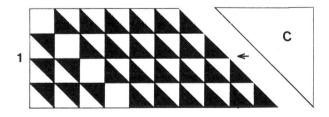

Then join them in rows (see piecing diagram B, steps 1 and 2), adding a square to each row, and ending each with a red triangle alone. Note that four white squares (template B) are needed for the rows in piecing diagram B, step 1.

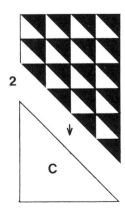

Once each group of four rows is completed and sewn together in the proper order, add a muslin triangle (C) to each group of four, creating two rectangles. You have now completed the treetop.

To complete the base of each tree, you'll need two large (C) triangles, one red and one muslin; two red E triangles; a red square (F); and two muslin houses (D). Sew the E and F shapes together in mirror image, as shown in the diagram at right. Then join them to square F, and finish by attaching the two C triangles, one on either side. Once you've completed these steps, you'll have three manageable pieces (1, 2, and 3 of diagram B). Sew 2 and 3 together, and then both to 1: the block is then completed.

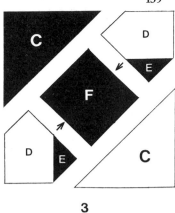

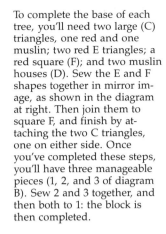

3

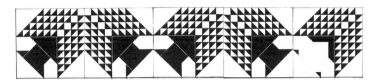

Once all 42 blocks are finished, attach them in horizontal rows of six blocks each, alternating the diagonal trees from left to right, as shown above. (For reasons of space, only five of the blocks appear here.) When you've pieced seven rows of blocks, invert every other row so that the tips of the trees' bases or the tops will "touch." Sew the rows together, and complete the quilt with a border and quilting stitch of your choice.

ACKNOWLEDGMENTS

I WOULD LIKE especailly to thank the many friends who offered unflagging encouragement and sincere interest in the preparation of this book: Marcia Berman and Paul Berbarian for their unbridled enthusiasm; Susan Frame, Susan Freeman, and Susan Gray for their nurturing personal and professional wisdom; Howard Gordon for his scholarly zeal and perfect discoveries; Deborah Harding for her imaginative leads and impressive follow-up; Lynn Lorwin for her good-humored perspective; Rita Rosencranz for her literary secrets; Jane Rosamilia, Rita and Jack Sacks, and Avis Skinner for their warm support and insights; and the twins, the Shandells, and especially the Fishers for cheerleading. And thanks to Larry Grow, Martin Greif, Frank Mahood, and especially Vicki Brooks of Main Street, who shared several lifetimes' knowledge about publishing, and to Lynda Duke for showing us how to re-create optical illusions.

Thanks also to those colleagues and friends who were so ready to share ideas and quilts to make this a rich study: Darwin D. Bearley, Judi Boisson, Susan Parrish, Jolise Kelter and Michael Malce, Michael Council, Sandra Mitchell, Judith and James Milne, Stella Rubin, Barbara Mintz and Rusty Ettinger, Shelley Zegart, Julie Silber, Elizabeth Enfield, Frank Ames, Bets Ramsey, Barbara Janos, Amy Finkel, Morgan Anderson, Tom Foster, Blanche Greenstein and Thomas Woodard, Harris Diamant and Norman Brosterman, and Robert Bishop.

Quilts or photographs have been provided by the following individuals and organizations:

Frank Ames, New York; Morgan Anderson, Frederick, Md.; Darwin D. Bearley, Akron, Ohio; Judi Boisson Antique American Quilts, New York, Westport, Conn., and Southampton, N.Y.; Buckboard Antiques, Oklahoma City; Michael Council, Columbus, Ohio; The Esprit Collection of Esprit de Corp., San Francisco and owner/collector Doug Tompkins, curator Julie Silber, and photographers Sharon Risedorph and Lynn Kellner; M. Finkel & Daughter, Philadelphia; The Fosters, Pittsfield, Ill.; Guernsey's, New York; Barbara S. Janos and Barbara Ross, New York; Kelter-Malce, New York; The Kentucky Museum, Western Kentucky University, Bowling Green and curator Christian Carron; The Kentucky Quilt Project, Inc., Louisville and director Shelley Zegart and coordinator Dorothy West; Paula Laverty, Brooklyn, N.Y.; The Museum of American Folk Art, New York and director Robert Bishop, curator Elizabeth Warren, and photography coordinator Karla Friedlich; Judith and James Milne, New York; Owensboro Area Museum, Owensboro, Ky.; Susan Parrish, New York; The Quilt Digest Press, San Francisco; Quilts of Tennessee, Chattanooga and director Bets Ramsey; Stella Rubin, Potomac, Md.; Tewksbury Antiques, Oldwick, N.J.; Vis-a-Vis, Nantucket, Mass.; and Eva and David Wheatcroft, Lewisburg, Pa.

BIBLIOGRAPHY

ALBERS, JOSEF. *Interaction of Color.* New Haven: Yale University Press, 1963.

ALLEN, JEANNE. *Designer's Guide to Color 3.* San Francisco: Chronicle Books, 1986.

ARNHEIM, RUDOLF. *Art and Visual Perception.* 2nd ed. Berkeley: University of California Press, 1974.

BISHOP, ROBERT AND ELIZABETH SAFANDA. *A Gallery of Amish Quilts.* New York: E. P. Dutton, 1976.

BISHOP, ROBERT, WILLIAM SECORD, AND JUDITH REITER WEISSMAN. *Quilts, Coverlets, Rugs & Samplers.* New York: Alfred A. Knopf, 1982.

BRESENHAN, KAROLINE PATTERSON AND NANCY O'BRYANT PUENTES. *Lone Stars, A Legacy of Texas Quilts, 1836-1936.* Austin: University of Texas Press, 1986.

CARRAHER, RONALD G. *Optical Illusions and the Visual Arts.* New York: Van Nostrand Reinhold, 1966.

COLBY, AVERIL. *Patchwork.* New York: Charles Scribner's Sons, 1958.

DEWHURST, C. KURT, BETTY MacDOWELL, AND MARSHA MacDOWELL. *Artists in Aprons.* New York: E. P. Dutton in association with The Museum of American Folk Art, 1979.

DUKE, DENNIS AND DEBORAH HARDING. *America's Glorious Quilts.* New York: Hugh Lauter Levin Associates, 1987.

DURANT, STUART. *Ornament.* New York: Overlook Press, 1986.

EARLE, ALICE MORSE. *Home Life in Colonial Days.* 1898. Reprint. Middle Village, N.Y.: Jonathan David Publishers, 1975.

ERNST, BRUNO. *The Magic Mirror of M. C. Escher.* New York: Ballantine Books, 1976.

FAIRFIELD, HELEN. *Patchwork from Mosaics.* New York: Arco Publishing, 1985.

FALES, DEAN A., JR. *American Painted Furniture.* 1972. Reprint. New York: Bonanza Books, 1986.

FINLEY, JOHN AND JONATHAN HOLSTEIN. *Kentucky Quilts 1800-1900.* Washington, D.C.: Dicmar Publishing, 1982.

FINLEY, RUTH E. *Old Patchwork Quilts and the Women Who Made Them.* Reprint. Newton Centre, Mass.: Charles T. Branford Company, 1983.

FOX, SANDI. *19th Century American Patchwork Quilt.* Tokyo: The Seibu Museum of Art, 1983.

HADERS, PHYLLIS. *The Main Street Pocket Guide to Quilts.* Pittstown, N.J.: The Main Street Press, 1983.

_____. *Sunshine & Shadow: The Amish and their Quilts.* Rev. ed. Pittstown, N.J.: The Main Street Press, 1984.

HALL, CARRIE A. AND ROSE G. KRETSINGER. *The Romance of the Patchwork Quilt in America.* New York: Bonanza Books, 1935.

HINSON, DOLORES A. *Quilting Manual.* New York: Dover Publications, 1980.

HOCHBERG, JULIAN E. *Perception.* 2nd ed. Englewood Cliffs, N.J.: Prentice-Hall, 1978.

HOLSTEIN, JONATHAN. *The Pieced Quilt: An American Design Tradition.* Greenwich, Conn.: New York Graphic Society, 1975.

HORTON, ROBERTA. *Calico and Beyond: The Use of Patterned Fabric in Quilts.* Lafayette, Calif.: C & T Publishing, 1987.

ICKIS, MARGUERITE. *The Standard Book of Quiltmaking and Collecting.* New York: Dover Publications, 1949.

IRWIN, JOHN RICE. *A People and Their Quilts.* Exton, Pa.: Schiffer Publishing, 1984.

JONES, OWEN. *The Grammar of Ornament.* 1856. Reprint. London, England: Studio Editions of Bestseller Publications, 1986.

JUSTEMA, WILLIAM. *The Pleasures of Pattern.* New York: Van Nostrand Reinhold, 1982.

KILE, MICHAEL AND RODERICK KIRACOFE, EDS. *The Quilt Digest.* 5 vols. San Francisco: The Quilt Digest Press, 1983-87.

KOBAYASHI, KEI. *Encyclopedia of American Patchwork Quilts: A Loving Study.* Tokyo: Bunka Publishing Company, 1983.

_____. *How to Make Geometric Patterns by Origami.* Tokyo: Bunka Publishing Company, 1986.

_____. *Shelburne Museum: The Quilt.* Tokyo: Gakken Publishing Company, 1986.

KOLTER, JANE BENTLEY. *Forget Me Not: A Gallery of Friendship and Album Quilts.* Pittstown, N.J.: The Main Street Press, 1985.

KUEPPERS, HARALD. *The Basic Law of Color Theory.* Woodbury, N.Y.: Barron's, 1980.

LASANSKY, JEANNETTE. *In the Heart of Pennsylvania: 19th & 20th Century Quiltmaking Traditions.* Lewisburg, Pa.: Oral Traditions Project, 1985.

LEWIS, PHILIPPA AND GILLIAN DARLEY. *Dictionary of Ornament.* New York: Pantheon Books, 1986.

LIPMAN, JEAN. *Provocative Parallels.* New York: E. P. Dutton, 1975.

LIPMAN, JEAN AND ALICE WINCHESTER. *The Flowering of American Folk Art (1776-1876).* New York: The Viking Press, 1974.

McKIM, RUBY. *One Hundred and One Patchwork Patterns.* Rev. ed. New York: Dover Publications, 1962.

MONTGOMERY, FLORENCE M. *Textiles in America: 1650-1870.* New York: W. W. Norton & Company, 1984.

NELSON, CYRIL I. AND CARTER HOUCK. *Treasury of American Quilts.* New York: Greenwich House, 1982.

ORLOFSKY, PATSY AND MYRON. *Quilts in America.* New York: McGraw-Hill Book Company, 1974.

ROSE, BARBARA. *American Art Since 1900.* Rev. & exp. ed. New York: Holt, Rinehart & Winston, 1975.

SAFFORD, CARLETON AND ROBERT BISHOP. *America's Quilts and Coverlets.* New York: E. P. Dutton, 1980.

STOCKTON, JAMES. *Designer's Guide to Color 2.* San Francisco: Chronicle Books, 1984.

THIEL, PHILIP. *Visual Awareness and Design.* Seattle: University of Washington Press, 1983.

TOMLONSON, JUDY SCHROEDER. *Mennonite Quilts and Pieces.* Intercourse, Pa.: Good Books, 1985.

WALKER, MICHELLE. *The Complete Book of Quiltmaking.* New York: Alfred A. Knopf, 1986.

WIEN, CAROL ANNE. *The Great American Log Cabin Quilt Book.* New York: E. P. Dutton, 1984.

WONG, WUCIUS. *Principles of Color Design.* New York: Van Nostrand Reinhold, 1987.